I

STUDY GUIDE
for
END TIMES
and
1000 YEARS OF PEACE

by
Melissa Redpill The World
FreedomForce.LIVE

CONTENTS

PREFACE

The Book of Revelation is complicated. I guess that's an understatement.

The Revelation is chock full of intricate symbolism. It's loaded with wonders in the heavens. It has references to many obscure Biblical texts. Plus, most everyone has a misunderstanding of End Times because modern teaching has led us all on a wild goose chase! (I think it was intentional.) But on top of all of that, the Lord told Daniel He was going to seal up the vision and only reveal it at the "end." So, don't feel bad if after listening to the videos, and reading the books, and listening to the audiobook on "End Times and 1000 Years of Peace," you still don't feel you have a firm handle on this very complex part of God's Word.

Still, with all of that said, it is **very important** that we understand this wonderful revelation the LORD gave us! For those who have been in the Freedom Force Battalion, I'm sure you would agree that knowing the truth that this is the End Times for the New World Order satanic cabal, and that we will soon enter 1000 years of peace on earth, has kept you in peace during this epic Battle of Armageddon. Just imagine if you still thought the world was going to be destroyed and we were going to escape earth and leave loved ones behind! The modern-day end times teaching is horrible!

If you are new to the Freedom Force Battalion, get ready! The truth about Revelation is quite different from what many of us were led to believe. But everything you will learn actually fits with the Word of God and doesn't leave puzzle pieces leftover! It's very good news… Because our future is so bright with our Lord Jesus as the King of the Millennial Kingdom on earth!

That is why I am assembling this study guide. I want to help everyone to understand this wonderful revelation backward and forward so you will stay encouraged, and be able to help those around you to be filled with hope and anticipation too!

Of course you can do the study guide on your own. And you can do the study guide while you watch the Small Group Study Guide videos we created on *FreedomForce.LIVE*. And even better still, you can use this Study Guide in small groups with those who are hungry to understand the wonderful truth about End Times! Either way, I hope this is a blessing to you. The LORD promised that those who study the book of Revelation will be blessed. Now we know why! It is critical to understand this critical information at this critical moment in history!

I encourage you to read "End Times and 1000 Years of Peace" first. Then try to complete the Study Guide without peeking at the teacher guide answer key. Part of the excitement of the Book of the Revelation is uncovering these nuggets of gold. It's the LORD'S glory to reveal a matter. And that's what He's done for us! Each lesson should be an adequate portion for a one week small group session. I know you will enjoy the LORD uncovering Revelation for you, as He did for me!

To whom much is given, much is required. We've been blessed with this understanding, so it is incumbent upon us to pass along the Good News of the Kingdom to those who have ears to hear.

We're praying the Lord will use us all to accomplish this very important assignment! Have fun! Enjoy! We are witnessing with our very own eyes what angels and prophets wished to see.

Love,
Melly
FreedomForce.LIVE

1-THE 6 STAGES OF END TIMES

You are going to love understanding the book of the Revelation!

If you have attempted to study Revelation before and were confused, don't worry.

This is going to be so easy…and everything will make sense!

This first chapter is a great way to start!

This will be a short summary of End Times so you have a framework of where we are going.

It might be different from what you have learned before, but just hang in there and you will see all the puzzle pieces come into place! We will go into more detail on these amazing Scripture passages in this Study Guide. This chapter is just a brief summary.

This chart represents the Biblical order of events in the book of the Revelation.

TRIBULATION

Don't think Nuclear Holocaust.

Think Wars.
Think Pandemic.
Think Financial Devastation.
Think Deception.
All brought to you courtesy of the New (Naaazi) World Order cabal.

> Matthew 24
> *21 "For there will be greater anguish than at any time since the world began.*
> *And it will never be so great again.*
> *22 In fact, unless that time of calamity is shortened, not a single person will survive.*
> *But it will be shortened for the sake of God's chosen ones."*

1. Humanity has been under a barrage of attacks for a long time, ramping up significantly in the past seven years: from the deception to the wars and rumors of wars, to the financial crises, to the pandemic, to the constant "1984" psyops. Was this the tribulation you expected? Explain.

For most of my life I was told Christians would be gone during the Tribulation, which would be *worldwide nuclear holocaust. I didn't know what to expect, because I didn't really buy into the* *narrative. I didn't expect deception from every side, and the worldwide political uprisings, and* *the pandemic and cancel culture. We were kept asleep on purpose until the time was right.*

GREAT AWAKENING

Of course, not everyone is awake. But clearly the Great Awakening is happening.

Ezekiel 37 tells us about an exceeding great army! This great army awakening is also talked about in Joel 2 and in Revelation 11. The LORD promised that when the time was right, He would awaken His warriors to fight, Fight, FIGHT! He would let us know who our true enemies were and lead His army in the fight to remove the evildoers from power.

Here are a few Scripture passages that prophesied about the Great Awakening.

> Ezekiel 37
> *9 "Then he said to me, "Speak a prophetic message to the winds, son of man. Speak a* *prophetic message and say, 'This is what the Sovereign Lord says: Come, O breath, from the* *four winds! Breathe into these dead bodies so they may live again.'"*
> *10 So I spoke the message as he commanded me, and breath came into their bodies. They all* *came to life and stood up on their feet - a great army."*

2. Do you feel that the breath of God breathed into you, and you stood up and joined the

fight?

Yes, I remember the day before the LORD awakened me. And then, by a miracle of His Spirit, I began to understand what was happening and had a voracious appetite to learn and to expose the truth. There is no doubt God breathed this life into me, and so many others have had the same experience at the same time! Just as He said!

BATTLE OF ARMAGEDDON

News Flash. We are currently fighting the Great Battle of Armageddon. Yep. That's why this is such a wild time for humanity.

Thankfully, this is not a tactile battle in the Middle East, as we thought. No. No. This is much bigger than that. We are not waging war against each other. We are waging war against the New World Order criminal cabal. We are exposing them and bringing them down, bit by bit, day after day after day. We could not have imagined this digital battle any more than John could have. We are literally fighting from our mobile phones and laptops.

The truth is setting us free. We are fighting with the sword of truth. We are fighting for the minds of our fellow brainwashed captives. And the New World Order has not been able to stop His truth from marching on, no matter how hard they have tried.

> Joel 2
> *7 "The attackers march like warriors and scale city walls like soldiers.*
> *Straight forward they march, never breaking rank.*
> *8 They never jostle each other; each moves in exactly the right position.*
> *They break through defenses without missing a step.*
> *9 They swarm over the city and run along its walls.*
> *They enter all the houses, climbing like thieves through the windows."*

3. How are we falling on the sword and not being wounded, digitally?

Our battlefield is social media. When we get "killed" off one platform, we just go to another platform and keep on exposing the truth!

4. How are we entering in at the windows?

We are sharing the truth in the digital battlefield with people we will likely never meet face to face. Our posts can reach them anywhere… even inside the privacy of their homes! Amazing!

MILLENNIAL REIGN OF CHRIST

The Bible gives us several glimpses into the beautiful future on earth that is coming soon! The Beast, False Prophet, and satan will be cast out. And we will have Health! Wealth! Peace! And Christ will rule on earth! Himself! Jesus told us to pray, "Your Kingdom come, Your will be done on earth as it is in Heaven." He meant it!

5. Write down a Bible verse that tells us of our bright future without wars. (you can use Isaiah 2, if you like.)

"The Lord will mediate between nations, and will settle international disputes.

They will hammer their swords into plowshares and their spears into pruning hooks.

Nation will no longer fight against nation, nor train for war anymore." (Isaiah 2:4 NLT)

6. Write down a Bible verse that tells us of our bright future of health and longevity. (you can use Isaiah 65:20, if you like.)

"No longer will babies die when only a few days old.

No longer will adults die before they have lived a full life.

No longer will people be considered old at one hundred!" (Isaiah 65:20 NLT)

7. Write down a Bible verse that tells us of our bright future with worldwide financial stability. (you can use Proverbs 13:22, if you like.)

"Suddenly, your debtors will take action. They will turn on you and take all you have, while you stand trembling and helpless. Because you have plundered many nations, now all the survivors will plunder you." (Habakkuk 2:7-8 NLT)

8. Write down a Bible verse that tells us of our bright future with Christ as King, living with us on earth.(you can use Zephaniah 3:15, if you like.)

"For the Lord will remove his hand of judgment and will disperse the armies of your enemy. And the Lord himself, the King of Israel, will live among you! At last your troubles will be over, and you will never again fear disaster." (Zephaniah 3:15 NLT)

These events clearly have not yet occurred. But they are coming soon!

Why doesn't the modern church talk about this?

GOG AND MAGOG BATTLE

After the Millennial Reign of Christ on earth, when the Beast, False Prophet, and satan have been cast out for 1,000 years, something shocking happens. Satan is allowed out of the pit to deceive humanity. I told you it was shocking!

The reason is that during the Millennial Kingdom, there will still be death. Our LORD Jesus promised to end death completely! So, when satan is allowed out of the pit, humanity will have one final battle. That battle, which is hardly ever talked about, is called the Gog and Magog Battle.

> Revelation 20
> 8 "He will go out to deceive the nations—called Gog and Magog—in every corner of the earth. He will gather them together for battle—a mighty army, as numberless as sand along the seashore.
> 9 "And I saw them as they went up on the broad plain of the earth and surrounded God's people and the beloved city. But fire from heaven came down on the attacking armies and consumed them."
> 10 "Then the devil, who had deceived them, was thrown into the fiery lake of burning sulfur, joining the beast and the false prophet. There they will be tormented day and night forever and ever."

To be honest that sounds really scary.

Being surrounded by demons?!!

Fire from heaven?!!

We will have 1,000 years' reprieve on earth, so we don't need to worry about that today! The satanic attack will come unexpectedly as humanity will have been enjoying 1,000 years of peace! I think the fire that comes down from God out of heaven that devours the demons is the fervent heat described in 2 Peter 3:10. The same fire that casts the demons into hell, also makes righteous humanity and the entire earth incorruptible!

> 2 Peter 3
> 10 "But the day of the Lord will come as unexpectedly as a thief. Then the heavens will pass away with a terrible noise, and the very elements themselves will disappear in fire, and the earth and everything on it will be found to deserve judgment."

Just imagine it! Satan GONE FOREVER!

NO MORE DEATH!

Heaven and Earth UNITED!

The LORD will make His home among all His people because Heaven and Earth merge!

NEW HEAVEN AND NEW EARTH

Revelation 21

1 *"Then I saw a new heaven and a new earth, for the old heaven and the old earth had disappeared. And the sea was also gone.*

2 And I saw the holy city, the new Jerusalem, coming down from God out of heaven like a bride beautifully dressed for her husband.

3 I heard a loud shout from the throne, saying, "Look, God's home is now among his people! He will live with them, and they will be his people. God himself will be with them.

4 "He will wipe every tear from their eyes, and there will be no more death or sorrow or crying or pain. All these things are gone forever.

5 And the one sitting on the throne said, "Look, I am making everything new!" And then he said to me, "Write this down, for what I tell you is trustworthy and true."

9. Write a Bible verse about the beautiful New Heaven and the New Earth. (you can use Revelation 21:1-3, if you like.)

"Then I saw a new heaven and a new earth, for the old heaven and the old earth had disappeared. And the sea was also gone. And I saw the holy city, the new Jerusalem, coming down from God out of heaven like a bride beautifully dressed for her husband. I heard a loud shout from the throne, saying, "Look, God's home is now among his people! He will live with them, and they will be his people. God himself will be with them." (Revelation 21:1-3 NLT)

I hope you enjoyed that short summary of End Times, and the puzzle is forming!
Next we will do another summary... this time a longer summary of the Book of Revelation.
One piece at a time, this amazing puzzle will start to come together!
Hang in there!

2-THE REVELATION DECODE

Here it is!
A brief decode of the outline of the Book of Revelation!
This took a lot of research… so enjoy!

Don't worry if it is difficult to take in on your first pass through. We will go through the Revelation piece by piece in this Study Guide, and you will love it! End Times will finally make sense! And it's GREAT NEWS FOR US!

THE REVELATION

> **Greetings and Doxology** (Chapter 1:1-8)
> **Jesus among the Seven Churches** (Chapter 1:9-20)
>> The seven stars symbolize those who love the LORD… His Bride.
>> The Revelation is about Jesus rescuing His Bride from the evil ones.
>
> **The Letters to the Seven Churches** (Chapters 2 and 3)
>> **Jesus warns His Bride about the synagogue of satan** - Chapters 2:9 and 3:9
>
> **The Throne, the Scroll and the Lamb** (Chapters 4 and 5)
>> **The Throne in Heaven** (Chapter 4)
>> All of heaven and earth worship the LORD
>> **The Seven-Sealed Scroll** (Chapter 5:1-5)
>> Our LORD Jesus alone is able to unseal the Revelation
>> **The Lamb Slain** (Chapter 5:6-14)
>> Jesus is worthy to save humanity through His blood alone.
>
> **The Seven Seals & God's People** (Chapter 6:1; 8:1)
>> Think of UNSEALING hidden information.
>> **First Seal: The White Horse** (Chapter 6:1-2)
>> The cabal rules humanity through puppet leaders.
>> **Second Seal: The Red Horse** (Chapter 6:3-4)
>> The cabal rules humanity by war and bloodshed.
>> **Third Seal: The Black Horse** (Chapter 6:5-6)
>> The cabal oppresses humanity by controlling the financial markets and currency.
>> **Fourth Seal: The Pale Horse** (Chapter 6:7-8)
>> The cabal destroys humanity using disease and drugs.
>> **Fifth Seal: The Souls under the Altar** (Chapter 6:9-11)

The LORD will answer all the prayers of the righteous made throughout all time. Their suffering will be avenged!

Sixth Seal: The Great Earthquake (Chapter 6:12-17)
Justice will be meted out on the wicked!

The Sealing of the 144,000 Army (Chapter 7:1-8)
These seals are the protection and guidance of the Holy Spirit on God's army.

The Great Multitude (Chapter 7:9-17)
This is all the believers awaiting the deliverance of humanity.

Seventh Seal: Silence in Heaven (Chapter 8:1)
The LORD waited until the Gospel had gone throughout the earth before He awakened His army to fight the evildoers.

The Seven Trumpets (Chapter 8:2;11:19)
The angels are not destroying the earth. The angels are revealing to humanity WHO has been destroying the earth, and HOW.

Introduction (Chapter 8:2-5)
The LORD is delivering humanity in response to our prayers.

First Trumpet: 33% Destruction of Trees and Grass (Chapter 8:6-7)
Secret Societies are destroying the strong and the weak.

Second Trumpet: 33% Destruction of the Sea (Chapter 8:8-9)
Secret Societies are destroying humanity worldwide indiscriminately.

Third Trumpet: 33% Destruction of Rivers and Fountains (Chapter 8:10-11)
Secret Societies are destroying life-giving water resources.

Fourth Trumpet: 33% Destruction of Sun, Moon, Stars (Chapter 8:12-13)
Secret Societies are destroying the air quality and hiding the heavenly signs.

Fifth Trumpet: The Plague of Locusts (Chapter 9:1-12)
Secret Societies are deceiving the masses using fake news.

Sixth Trumpet: Release of the Four Angels (Chapter 9:13-21)
The holy angels and God's Army have been released to destroy the evildoers!

The Angel and the Little Scroll (Chapter 10)
John gets redpilled by the Angel's Trumpets

The Two Witnesses (Chapter 11:1-14)
The Church and State were hijacked by the NWO cabal until God awakened us.

Seventh Trumpet: Hallelujah Chorus (Chapter 11:15-19)
Praise the LORD for coming to rule the earth!

The Key Players and Events in the Book of the Revelation (Chapters 12-14)

The Woman and the Dragon (Chapter 12) The Sign of the Son of Man in the heavenly clock was the kickoff to the Great Awakening and the Battle of Armageddon.

The Two Beasts (Chapter 13)
The LORD reveals the 1st Beast NWO cabal and the 2nd Beast False Prophets which include the demonic leadership of the religious institutions, the media, the government, etc. that deceive humanity into following the NWO cabal.

The Lamb and the 144,000 (Chapter 14:1-5)
Christ and His Army for the Battle of Armageddon.

The Harvest of the Earth (Chapter 14:6-20)
The Harvest of the Wicked and the Awakening of all of Humanity.

The Seven Bowls (Chapters 15 and 16)

Think of Bowls filled with God's Judgment on the NWO cabal.

The Song of Moses; Seven Angels with Seven Plagues (Chapter 15)

Interlude to Praise the LORD – Just and True are Thy Ways LORD!!

First Bowl: Painful Sores (Chapter 16:1-2)

The first judgments of exposure fall on the NWO cabal... panic strikes because they know what is coming.

Second Bowl: Sea Turns to Blood (Chapter 16:3)

The NWO cabal financial empire begins to crumble.

Third Bowl: Rivers and Springs of Water Become Blood (Chapter 16:4-7)

The NWO cabal and their minions crimes against children and their cannibalism is exposed.

Fourth Bowl: Sun Scorches People with Fire (Chapter 16:8-9)

Scorching Anger and Fear because everything they do to stop judgment backfires!

Fifth Bowl: Darkness (Chapter 16:10-11)

The NWO cabal's secret communication lines are exposed, causing them to not be able to communicate covertly. Extreme anger and frustration.

Sixth Bowl: Way of the Kings Prepared (Chapter 16:12-16)

The NWO cabal sees their empire slipping away, and that the meek will inherit the earth. This makes them angriest of all!

Seventh Bowl: Tremendous Earthquake (Chapter 16:17-21)

The Fall of the Cabal Babylon!

Babylon: The City of Evil (Chapter 17:1;19:5)

The Prostitute (Chapter 17)

How the evil NWO cabal uses the Harlot minions (controlled media, religion, education, medical, government officials, entertainment, banks, and technology) to run the world.

The Fall of Babylon (Chapter 18)

Pronouncement of the Destruction of NWO Babylon

Interlude to Praise the LORD

Praise for Babylon's Fall (Chapter 19:1-5)

Praise the LORD for destroying the Babylon NWO!

Praise for the Wedding of the Lamb (19:6-10)

Praise the LORD for saving His Bride!

Christ Destroys Babylon (Chapter 19:11-21)

Christ destroys Babylon and His army joins in the bloodbath!

Christ Begins to Rule Earth (Chapter 20:1-6)

The Beast, the False Prophet, and satan are cast into the bottomless pit, and humanity enjoys 1,000 years of Christ's reign on earth. Health, Wealth & Peace!

Gog & Magog Battle (Chapter 20:7-10)

satan is allowed out of the pit to deceive the nations. Then the LORD destroys satan, sin, and death forever!

Great White Throne Judgment (Chapter 20:11-15)

Humanity receives rewards according to their works.

New Heaven & New Earth (Chapter 21:1;22:5)

Heaven and Earth merge. Death, Sorrow, and Crying are no more!

Conclusion and Benediction (Chapter 22:6-21)

The beauty of Heaven and the Bride of Christ are revealed.

Yes…that was a lot! Even the summary was a lot to think through!

Let's briefly break it down to make sure you understand the high points from the summary above.

1. What do the four Horsemen reveal? (Revelation 6)

The cabal rules the world through puppet leaders, wars, financial oppression, and disease.

2. What do the Trumpets reveal? (Revelation 8)

The Trumpets reveal WHO is destroying the world and how they are doing it. The Trumps represent The Great Awakening.

3. Who do the Two Witnesses represent? (Revelation 11)

The Two Witnesses represent the Church and the State, which are supposed to bring justice to earth, but have been made useless due to NWO infiltration.

4. Who do the two Beasts represent? (Revelation 13)

The first beast represents the New World Order financial controllers who treat humanity like a giant game of Risk.

The second beast represents False Prophets which includes the demonic leadership of the religious institutions, the media, the government, etc. that deceive humanity into following the NWO cabal.

5. Who are the seven Bowls of God's judgment poured out on? (Revelation 15-16)

The bowls are filled with God's Judgment on the NWO cabal.

6. Who does the Harlot represent? (Revelation 17)

Harlot minions (controlled media, religion, education, medical, government officials, entertainment, banks, and technology) are used to run the world for the NWO.

7. What happens during the 1,000 years (Millennial Kingdom) discussed in Revelation 20?

The Beast, the False Prophet, and satan are cast into the bottomless pit, and humanity enjoys 1000 years of Christ's reign on earth. Health, Wealth & Peace!

8. After the Millennial Kingdom what Battle happens? (Revelation 20)

**satan is allowed out of the pit to deceive the nations. At the end of the Gog and Magog battle the LORD destroys satan, sin, and death forever!**

9. What happens to Heaven and Earth in Revelation 21?

**Heaven and Earth merge. Death, Sorrow, and Crying are no more!**

3-JESUS CHRIST IS THE VICTOR!

"End Times and 1000 Years of Peace" Chapter 1

Throughout these very strange times we are living in, our constant source of peace is this:
OUR LORD JESUS CHRIST IS THE VICTOR!
THE CHAMPION OF THE WORLD!
He will rule this earth and we can trust His perfect plan!

Let's start our Revelation Study Guide with that perspective, and we will be filled with hope and joy!
Below is the summary of the victory humanity is headed for!
WE ARE THE CHAMPIONS WITH CHRIST!

Isaiah 9:6-7	Christ's Kingdom will be established on earth
Revelation 5:1-5	Scroll
Genesis 49:9-10	Shiloh
Revelation 5:6	Christ the Lamb of God
Isaiah 53:7	Christ the Lamb of God
John 1:29	Jesus suffered for us and removed the world's guilt
Revelation 5:7-10	Jesus suffered for us and removed the world's guilt
Colossians 2:14-15	Christ's victory over satan
Revelation 17:14	Victory in the War of Armageddon
1 Peter 2:9	We are kings and priests
Isaiah 61:6	We will rule with Christ
Revelation 5:11	Jesus is the Ruler of the world
Daniel 7:10	Jesus is the Judge of the world
Revelation 5:12-13	Praise to Our Lord Jesus Christ
Daniel 7:13-14	Coronation of our Lord Jesus Christ

1. What does Isaiah 9 tell us about Christ and His Kingdom?

Isaiah 9 (TPT)

6"For unto us a child is born, unto us a son is given; And the government will be upon His shoulder.

7 And His name will be called Wonderful Counselor, Mighty God, Everlasting Father, Prince of Peace. Of the increase of His government and peace there will be no end.

Upon the throne of David and over His kingdom, To order it and establish it with judgment and justice From that time forward, even forever. The zeal of the Lord of hosts will perform this."

There will be no end to the increase of His righteous government and peace on earth. He will establish judgment and justice forever! Praise the LORD!

2. This passage is part of the Book of Revelation in the New Testament and describes John's vision of a scroll with seven seals that no one is able to open except for Jesus Christ. Clearly this passage refers to Jesus' role as the only one who can reveal God's plan and save humanity. What does this passage tell us about the desperate state of humanity?

Revelation 5 (TPT)

1 "Then I saw a scroll in the right hand of the one who was seated on the throne, a scroll written on both sides and sealed shut with seven seals.

2 And I saw a mighty angel who shouted with a loud voice, "Who is worthy to break the seals on this scroll and open it?"

3 But no one in heaven or on earth or beneath the earth was able to open the scroll and read its messages.

4 Then I began to weep bitterly because no one was found worthy to open the scroll and read it."

John knows humanity is ruined if there is no one who can reveal the truth to humanity and destroy the AntiChrist. Our struggle is against spiritual forces... literally demons. Humanity cannot defeat them, except by the power of Christ.

3. This verse is part of a larger passage that describes a vision of John in which he sees a scroll sealed with seven seals. No one in heaven or on earth is found worthy to open the scroll until Jesus Christ appears as the Lamb of God who was slain and resurrected. He takes the scroll from the right hand of God and begins to open its seals. The passage quoted is part of a song of praise that is sung by every creature in heaven and on earth to honor Jesus Christ for his sacrifice and redemption of humanity. What does Revelation 5 tell us of the hope that is found in our LORD Jesus Christ?

Revelation 5 (TPT)

5 *"Then one of the elders said to me, "Stop weeping. Look! The mighty Lion of Judah's tribe, the root of David—he has conquered! He is the worthy one who can open the scroll and its seven seals."*

Jesus is worthy! He has the power to save humanity! And He has the right to save humanity because of His accomplished work of salvation bearing our sins on the cross.

4. Who is Shiloh? And what is his role?

Genesis 49 (Amplified Classic version)

9 *"Judah, a lion's cub! With the prey, my son, you have gone high up [the mountain]. He stooped down, he crouched like a lion, And like a lion—who dares to rouse him?*

10 *The scepter [of royalty] shall not depart from Judah, Nor the ruler's staff from between his feet, Until Shiloh [the Messiah, the Peaceful One] comes to whom it belongs, And to him shall be the obedience of the peoples."*

This passage is part of Jacob's blessing to his sons before he died. He prophesied that Judah would be like a lion and that his descendants would rule over Israel. The scepter and ruler's staff refer to the symbols of authority and power that were used by kings in ancient times. The prophecy also speaks of the coming of Shiloh, who is believed by many to be a reference to Jesus Christ.

Shiloh is a name for Christ in his role as our righteous King! The Lion of the Tribe of Judah who has triumphed! He deserves the royal crown because He is the Son of God and because He paid the ransom for humanity with His own sinless, precious blood.

5. These passages are part of the prophecy of Isaiah about the suffering servant who would come to save us. Of course, this is a prophecy about our LORD Jesus. What was Christ's role in his first advent?

Revelation 5 (TPT)

6 *"Then I saw a young Lamb standing before the throne, encircled by the four living creatures and the twenty-four elders. He appeared to have been slaughtered but was now alive! He had seven horns and seven eyes, which are the seven Spirits of God sent out into all the earth."*

Isaiah 53 (TPT)

7 *"He was oppressed and harshly mistreated; still he humbly submitted, refusing to defend himself. He was led like a gentle lamb to be slaughtered. Like a silent sheep before his shearers, he didn't even open his mouth."*

Christ's role in His first advent was to put on human flesh and bear the guilt of the people, taking the punishment we deserved for sin and making us righteous in God's sight. He had to defeat satan at the cross, and fill the earth with His redeemed people, before He could cast satan from his earthly throne and out of this earth.

6. This is part of the Gospel of John and describes John the Baptist's testimony about our LORD Jesus Christ. Who did John recognize Jesus to be?

John 1 (TPT)

29 *"The very next day, John saw Jesus coming to him to be baptized, and John cried out, "Look! There he is—God's Lamb! He takes away the sin of the entire world!"*

John recognized our LORD Jesus as the One who would suffer and die for the sins of humanity.

7. Soak in Revelation 5:7-10. What is our purpose on earth for which Christ redeemed us?

Revelation 5

7 *"He came and took the scroll from the right hand of the one who sat on the throne.*

8 *And when he took it, the four living creatures and the twenty-four elders fell down before the Lamb. Each one had a harp and golden bowls filled with sweet fragrant incense, which are the prayers of God's holy ones. And they were all singing this new song of praise to the Lamb.*

9 *Because you were slaughtered for us, you are worthy to take the scroll and open its seals. Your blood was the price paid to redeem us. You purchased us to bring us to God out of every tribe, language, people group, and nation.*

10 *You have chosen us to serve our God and formed us into a kingdom of priests who reign on the earth."*

"You purchased us to bring us to God out of every tribe, language, people group, and nation. You have chosen us to serve our God and formed us into a kingdom of priests who reign on the earth."

Our purpose is to take the Kingdom of Christ by force and to rule the earth!

8. This verse is a reminder that through Jesus Christ, we have been forgiven of our sins and

reconciled with God. Our sins have been erased and we have been made new in Christ. Jesus has triumphed over the powers and principalities of darkness and has given us victory over sin and death. How does this truth impact your role on earth?

Colossians 2 (TPT)

14 "He canceled out every legal violation we had on our record and the old arrest warrant that stood to indict us. He erased it all—our sins, our stained soul—he deleted it all and they cannot be retrieved! Everything we once were in Adam has been placed onto his cross and nailed permanently there as a public display of cancellation.

15 Then Jesus made a public spectacle of all the powers and principalities of darkness, stripping away from them every weapon and all their spiritual authority and power to accuse us. And by the power of the cross, Jesus led them around as prisoners in a procession of triumph. He was not their prisoner; they were his!"

Jesus defeated satan at the cross and He will remove satan from his role as prince of the power of the air too! We are witnessing our LORD stripping away all their earthly authority through their minions the NWO. And we get to participate in His victory! We are making the evildoers a public spectacle!

9. This verse is part of a vision that John had in which he saw war between a woman riding on a beast (satanic forces on earth and their minions) and the Lamb (Jesus Christ and his followers). What is absolutely inevitable? And who is fighting alongside Christ?

Revelation 17 (TPT)

14 "Together they will make war against the Lamb, but the Lamb will conquer them, for he is Lord of lords and King of kings. And those who are with him are chosen and faithful."

The Lamb will conquer them because He is the King of kings. And we – the chosen and faithful – are fighting by His side. We are blessed of the LORD.

10. This verse is a reminder that we are all chosen by God to be His treasure and to serve Him. We are called to be a spiritual nation set apart for God's purposes. As His chosen people, we have been called out of darkness and into His marvelous light. We are His very own and have been redeemed by the blood of Jesus Christ. Let's take this opportunity to thank the LORD for this indescribable gift!

1 Peter 2 (TPT)

9 "But you are God's chosen treasure —priests who are kings, a spiritual "nation" set apart as God's devoted ones. He called you out of darkness to experience his marvelous light, and now he claims you as his very own. He did this so that you would broadcast his glorious wonders throughout the world."

Lord, we certainly don't deserve this amazing blessing to rule with You in Your holy Kingdom. We stand here by Your grace alone. You called us out of darkness into Your marvelous light so we could broadcast Your acclaim throughout the world. We will praise You forever and ever! We are so thankful you claim us as Your very own treasure.

11. This passage is part of the Book of Isaiah in the Old Testament and describes the blessings that God will bestow upon his people. Many Christians believe that this passage refers to the spiritual blessings that believers receive through faith in Jesus Christ. What does our future look like, patriots?

Isaiah 61 (TPT)

6 "You will be called Priests of Yahweh and called Ministers of our God. You will feast on the wealth of nations and revel in their riches."

We will live in a world of peace and prosperity that everyone will enjoy. The day of troubles will be OVER!

12. This passage is part of the Book of Revelation in the New Testament and describes John's vision of a multitude of angels worshiping Jesus Christ. Imagine and try to put into words what the earth will be like when the satanic forces are gone, and everyone worships Christ!

Revelation 5 (TPT)

11 "Then I looked, and I heard the voices of thousands and millions of angels surrounding the throne and the living creatures and the elders. They sang in a mighty chorus: "Worthy is the Lamb who was slaughtered— to receive power and riches and wisdom and strength and honor and glory and blessing.

12 And as I watched, all of them were singing with thunderous voices: "Worthy is Christ the Lamb who was slaughtered to receive great power and might, wealth and wisdom, and honor, glory, and praise!

13 Then I heard every creature in heaven and on earth, in the underworld and on the sea —all that lives—singing these words: "Blessing, honor, glory, and power belong to the one sitting on the throne and to the Lamb forever and ever!"

I envision everyone finally understanding the truth about what our LORD Jesus did to defeat the evil that has overtaken the world. I can see the relief on their faces when they realize all the evil and deception and wars and sickness and lack are GONE! Amazement and joy and wonder will fill everyone as they realize the world was set free by our LORD Jesus Himself! Imagine their wonder that He judged the wicked and rescued even those who were brainwashed into fighting against Him! True Love!

13. This passage is part of the Book of Daniel in the Old Testament and describes Daniel's vision of a heavenly court where God sits in judgment over the nations. One day, every man, woman, and child will stand before the White Throne Judgment. How does impact your view of humanity, and your daily life?

> Daniel 7 (TPT)
>
> *10 "A river of fire flowed from his presence. Thousands upon thousands served him; ten thousand times ten thousand stood before him. The court was convened, and the books were opened."*

The river of fire symbolize white hot justice! Jesus rules from this throne and will judge the wicked. I'm very glad He saved me and I'm on His side!

14. This passage is part of a vision that Daniel had in which he saw four beasts with represent four kingdoms. The son of man is a figure who represents the people of God and is given authority over all nations. What does this passage tell us about the inevitability of Christ's Kingdom on earth?

> Daniel 7 (TPT)
>
> *13 "As I continued to watch this vision of the night, I suddenly saw one like a son of man coming with the clouds of heaven. He approached the Ancient of Days and was led into his presence.*
>
> *14 He was given authority, honor, and sovereignty over all the nations of the world, so that people of every race and nation and language would obey him. His rule is eternal—it will never end. His kingdom will never be destroyed."*

"People of every race and nation and language will obey him. His rule is eternal—it will never end. His kingdom will never be destroyed." That's why Nothing Can Stop What Is Coming!

As we dive in to the very complex passages about End Times, let's keep this wonderful truth in our hearts. We are headed to a future on earth with Christ recognized as King, and with His followers ruling and reigning with Him! Peace and health and wealth on earth!

How in the world can we bring all of humanity together under Christ? That's what Study Guide #4 is all about!

4-WAITING ON A MESSIAH

"End Times and 1000 Years of Peace" Chapter 2

Let's look at the BIG PICTURE of where the world is headed.
The entire world is waiting on a Messiah to rescue humanity.

1. Write the name of the Messiah for each world religion.

Followers of Judaism are waiting on their **MESHIACH.**

Followers of Christianity are waiting on their **MESSIAH.**

Followers of Hinduism are waiting on their **KRISHNA.**

Followers of Buddhism are waiting on their **MAITREYA.**

Followers of Islam are waiting on their **MAHDI.**

2. Describe the fulfillment of this verse:

> Ephesians 2
> *14 "For Christ himself has brought peace to us. He united Jews and Gentiles into one people when, in his own body on the cross, he broke down the wall of hostility that separated us. 15 He did this by ending the system of law with its commandments and regulations. He made peace between Jews and Gentiles by creating in himself one new people from the two groups."*

Christ will unite people all over the world. All people will recognize him as their Messiah! There will be no more division over religion!

Imagine all the world religions coming together as one under Christ. Every knee will bow and every tongue will confess that Jesus Christ is LORD.

3. Let's briefly tackle the terminology of the word Jew. For more on this, see the Addendum

in "End Times and 1000 Years of Peace."

The word Jew is used in many ways, which has caused great confusion. On purpose.

Always read the passage for context to determine the meaning.

Place a checkmark for all that are technically Jews:

X True Believers in Christ

X A person with a physical lineage of Judah.

___ A person who has hijacked the name Jew for evil purposes. (Revelation 3:9)

X Judahite believers in Christ (Messianic Jews)

X All of those who follow God from their heart.

Do you see how this can be confusing?

4. Describe these verses in your own words.

> Romans 2
> 28 *"For you are not a true Jew just because you were born of Jewish parents or because you have gone through the ceremony of circumcision.*
> 29 *No, a true Jew is one whose heart is right with God. And true circumcision is not merely obeying the letter of the law; rather, it is a change of heart produced by the Spirit. And a person with a changed heart seeks praise from God, not from people."*

> Galatians 3
> 28 *"There is no longer Jew or Gentile, slave or free, male and female. For you are all one in Christ Jesus."*

I am a true Jew. Not because of my ethnicity or a ceremony. I am a true Jew because my heart is right with God, because His Spirit dwells within me. Our status in Christ supersedes any other distinction… ethnicity, social status, or gender.

5. Underline the parts of these Bible verses that cause Christians to expect Christ's return to earth.

> John 14
> 3 *"When everything is ready, I will come again and receive you to Myself; that where I am there you may be also."* (NKJV)

> Matthew 25
> 31 *"But when the Son of Man comes in his glory, and all the angels with him, then he will sit upon his glorious throne.*

32 All the nations will be gathered in his presence, and he will separate the people as a shepherd separates the sheep from the goats.
33 He will place the sheep at his right hand and the goats at his left."

Matthew 24
3 "Later, Jesus sat on the Mount of Olives. His disciples came to him privately and said, "Tell us, when will all this happen? <u>What sign will signal your return and the end of the world?</u>"

Titus 2
13 "While Jesus we look forward with hope to <u>that wonderful day when the glory of our great God and Savior, Jesus Christ, will be revealed.</u>"

6. Next let's look at why Christians are expecting the imminent return of Christ.

First of all, Jesus promised He would be with us even until the end of the AGE. An AGE is 2,000 years.
Our LORD Jesus was answering their question by telling them his return and the Tribulation / Battle of Armageddon would take place during the transition from the Age of Pisces to the Age of Aquarius.
So it stands to reason that our LORD'S return is now!

NOTE – The Age of Pisces is the Church Age when we have been fishers of men. The Age of Aquarius is represented by a man pouring water out of a water pot, symbolizing the Holy Spirit pouring out His Spirit on all flesh!

Matthew 28
*20 "Teach these new disciples to obey all the commands I have given you. And be sure of this: I am with you always, even to the end of the **age**."*

Also, the prophet Daniel interpreted King Nebuchadnezzar's dream as depicting the kingdoms throughout history. We are down to the last kingdom, before the Millennial Kingdom!

Daniel Chapter 2

Babylonian Kingdom

36 "That was the dream. Now we will tell the king what it means.

37 Your Majesty, you are the greatest of kings. The God of heaven has given you sovereignty, power, strength, and honor.

38 He has made you the ruler over all the inhabited world and has put even the wild animals and birds under your control. You are the head of gold.""

Medo-Persian Empire and Greek Empire

39 "But after your kingdom comes to an end, another kingdom, inferior to yours, will rise to take your place. After that kingdom has fallen, yet a third kingdom, represented by bronze, will rise to rule the world."

Roman Empire

40 "Following that kingdom, there will be a fourth one, as strong as iron. That kingdom will smash and crush all previous empires, just as iron smashes and crushes everything it strikes."

Divided Kingdom

41 "The feet and toes you saw were a combination of iron and baked clay, showing that this kingdom will be divided. Like iron mixed with clay, it will have some of the strength of iron.

42 But while some parts of it will be as strong as iron, other parts will be as weak as clay.

43 This mixture of iron and clay also shows that these kingdoms will try to strengthen themselves by forming alliances with each other through intermarriage. But they will not hold together, just as iron and clay do not mix."

The Divine Kingdom

44 "During the reigns of those kings, the God of heaven will set up a kingdom that will never be destroyed or conquered. It will crush all these kingdoms into nothingness, and it will stand forever.

45 That is the meaning of the rock cut from the mountain, though not by human hands, that crushed to pieces the statue of iron, bronze, clay, silver, and gold. The great God was showing the king what will happen in the future. The dream is true, and its meaning is certain."

What in Nebuchadnezzar's dream leads us to believe the return of Christ is imminent?

__All the kingdoms of this world have come and gone, except for the divided kingdom New World Order. Next is the divine kingdom which will never end!__

7. On the statue, what body part are we down to, according to the timeline of earthly kingdoms?

__The toes!__

8. What will be setup when Christ returns?

__The God of heaven will set up a kingdom that will never be destroyed or conquered.__

9. What does the stone in Daniel 2:45 do?

__It will crush to pieces all the other kingdoms!__

10. Who does the stone in Daniel 2:45 represent?

__Our LORD Jesus Christ!__

11. There is another prophecy in Daniel 7 about the evil empires/kingdoms. This prophecy depicts four empires...progressively more ruthless against humanity. I believe these are modern empires and the final monster is an unrecognizable conglomeration of evil tyranny. I believe the lion represents the United Kingdom, the bear represents Russia, the leopard represents the Nazi Regime, but that is speculation. I am convinced the Dreadful Beast represents the worldwide criminal cabal AntiChrist New World Order.

Daniel 7
2 "In my vision that night, I, Daniel, saw a great storm churning the surface of a great sea, with strong winds blowing from every direction.
3 Then four huge beasts came up out of the water, each different from the others."

<u>LION</u>
4 The first beast was like a lion with eagles' wings. As I watched, its wings were pulled off, and it was left standing with its two hind feet on the ground, like a human being. And it was given a human mind."

<u>BEAR</u>
5 Then I saw a second beast, and it looked like a bear. It was rearing up on one side, and it had three ribs in its mouth between its teeth. And I heard a voice saying to it, "Get up! Devour the flesh of many people!"

<u>LEOPARD</u>
6 "Then the third of these strange beasts appeared, and it looked like a leopard. It had four bird's wings on its back, and it had four heads. Great authority was given to this beast."

<u>DREADFUL BEAST</u>
7 "Then in my vision that night, I saw a fourth beast—terrifying, dreadful, and very strong. It devoured and crushed its victims with huge iron teeth and trampled their remains beneath its feet. It was different from any of the other beasts, and it had ten horns.

8 As I was looking at the horns, suddenly another small horn appeared among them. Three of the first horns were torn out by the roots to make room for it. This little horn had eyes like human eyes and a mouth that was boasting arrogantly."

12. What in Daniel 7:7 correlates the Dreadful Beast as representing the New World Order cabal?

__Terrifying, Dreadful, Strong, Devouring and crushing victims and trampling them even after__

__they are dead. 10 horns like the 10 worldwide NWO authority divisions.__

13. How might the 10 horns of Daniel 2 correlate with the 10 toes of Daniel 7?

__They likely both represent the 10 worldwide divisions of the New World Order's power structure.__

14. What organization might the Little Horn represent, that even though it is small, is able to push everyone around?

__The Little Horn might represent the UN, but more likely and represents the nation we are not__

__allowed to talk about, which is the head of the New World Order. This group took the place of__

__domination from the British Empire, the Russian Empire, and the German Third Reich, and is__

__smaller but even more ruthless than they were. (Another name for horn is trump, as in the fake__

__little trump. Something to think about, along with the battle of Little Big Horn.)__

15. But Daniel's vision goes on to say the dreadful beast will be destroyed! Just like the evil empires were destroyed and the Kingdom of Christ was established on earth in Daniel's interpretation of Nebuchadnezzar's dream recorded in Daniel Chapter 2.

> Daniel 7
> *11 "I continued to watch because I could hear the little horn's boastful speech. I kept watching until the fourth beast was killed and its body was destroyed by fire.*
> *12 The other three beasts had their authority taken from them, but they were allowed to live a while longer.*
> *13 "As my vision continued that night, I saw someone like a son of man coming with the clouds of heaven. He approached the Ancient One and was led into his presence.*
> *14 He was given authority, honor, and sovereignty over all the nations of the world, so that people of every race and nation and language would obey him. His rule is eternal—it will never end. His kingdom will never be destroyed."*

According to these two prophecies, what is the future of the New World Order Beast?

Daniel 2 says "That kingdom will smash and crush all previous empires, just as iron smashes and crushes everything it strikes" and Daniel 7 says, "I kept watching until the fourth beast was killed and its body was destroyed by fire. That means the New World Order will be destroyed!

16. What does the future hold for humanity on earth?

Daniel 2 says "the God of heaven will set up a kingdom that will never be destroyed or conquered. It will crush all these kingdoms into nothingness, and it will stand forever." and Daniel 7 says " the Son of Man will be given authority and honor and sovereignty over all the nations of the world. His kingdom will never end!"

17. Identify the three current visible leaders of the New World Order AntiChrist cabal. See the end of Chapter 2.

Head of Financial Control *Rothschilds/Payseurs*

Head of Political Control *Soros*

Head of Human and Drug Trafficking Control *House of Saud which fell and is now run through DC.*

18. What is the structure the New World Order AntiChrist has used to accomplish their evil agenda, by promising "hidden knowledge" and power?

Secret Societies in a pyramid structure.

19. Most members of these groups are just minions and useful idiots of the NWO.

The ones near the top of the evil pyramid call themselves *"elite."*

Historically there have been 13 *bloodline* families that have amassed wealth and power like a worldwide game of Risk.

Next let's study several of the lies the NWO forced on humanity, so they could keep the masses brainwashed and deceived.

5-AWAKENING HUMANITY

"End Times and 1000 Years of Peace" Chapter 3

Ezekiel 37 & Joel 2

This very strange vision Ezekiel had gives us an amazing picture of what humanity is experiencing right now! Take a moment and read the entire vision recorded in Ezekiel 37.

> Ezekiel 37
> 1 *"The Lord took hold of me, and I was carried away by the Spirit of the Lord to a valley filled with bones.*
> 2 *He led me all around among the bones that covered the valley floor. They were **scattered** everywhere across the ground and were completely dried out."*

1. What is the significance of the bones?

The bones symbolize that humanity is as good as dead. They how no power or even any idea about how to save themselves from the New World Order.

2. What is the significance of the bones being scattered?

Scattered is a term used for the house of Israel scattered throughout the world... seemingly disorganized, not even knowing their own identity. But they LORD knows them and can raise them into His army easily!

3. What is the significance of the bones being on the valley?

They are in the lowest most debased position on earth. They are not in positions of power. They are easy prey for the NWO on the mountaintop.

> Ezekiel 37
> 3 *"Then he asked me, "Son of man, can these bones become living people again?"*
> *"O Sovereign Lord," I replied, "you alone know the answer to that."*

NOTE – "living people" or "to live again" means to be free people or to be free again.

4 "Then he said to me, "Speak a prophetic message to these bones and say, 'Dry bones, listen to the word of the Lord!
5 This is what the Sovereign Lord says: Look! I am going to put breath into you and make you live again!"
6 I will put flesh and muscles on you and cover you with skin. I will put breath into you, and you will come to life. Then you will know that I am the Lord.'"

4. Do you think it is odd for Ezekiel to speak to bones?

Yes. Humanly speaking, these bones cannot respond to Ezekiel.

5. Would you have felt silly speaking to bones in his vision?

Probably. But Ezekiel knew the LORD was able to do anything, as he said, "You alone know, LORD."

6. How does the LORD'S command to Ezekiel compare to sharing the Good News?

When we share the Gospel, we know that unbeliever is spiritually dead to God. But we also know the LORD is able to awaken them and give them new life!

> Ezekiel 37
> *7 "So I spoke this message, just as he told me. Suddenly as I spoke, there was a rattling noise all across the valley. The bones of each body came together and attached themselves as complete skeletons.*
> *8 Then as I watched, muscles and flesh formed over the bones. Then skin formed to cover their bodies, but they still had no breath in them."*

Ezekiel 37:7-8 is referenced in a similar passage in Revelation 11:11.

> Revelation 11
> *11 "But after three and a half days, God breathed life into them, and they stood up! Terror struck all who were staring at them."*

7. Wow! What a vision! What is the difference between the bones having skin and bones having breath?

Having skin on the bones indicates they are alive to God. They believe in the LORD and live Him.

But breath in them indicates they are chosen to rise up as His mighty army to fight Armageddon!

> Ezekiel 37
> *9 "Then he said to me, "Speak a prophetic message to the winds, son of man. Speak a prophetic message and say, 'This is what the Sovereign Lord says: Come, O breath, from the four winds! Breathe into these dead bodies so they may live again.'"*

8. Are Ezekiel 37 and Matthew 24 parallel passages about the Battle of Armageddon? In what way?

> Matthew 24
> *31 "And he will send out his angels with the mighty blast of a trumpet, and they will gather his chosen ones from all over the world—from the farthest ends of the earth and heaven."*

Recorded in Ezekiel 37 the LORD had Ezekiel speak to the breath to come breathe on the slain.

Recorded in Matthew 24 the LORD sent the angels to gather/awaken His chosen warriors. The results were identical. They woke up and became His mighty army!

> Ezekiel 37
> *10 "So I spoke the message as he commanded me, and breath came into their bodies. They all came to life and stood up on their feet—a great army."*

9. Who is this great army in Ezekiel's vision?

God hand-selected warriors from every nation and creed from all over the world, who are exposing the New World Order satanic criminal cabal in this epic Battle of Armageddon.

10. How does the army in Ezekiel's vision compare to the army in Joel Chapter 2?

> Joel 2
> *1 "Sound the trumpet in Jerusalem!*
> *Raise the alarm on my holy mountain!*
> *Let everyone tremble in fear*
> *because the day of the Lord is upon us.*
> *2 It is a day of darkness and gloom,*
> *a day of thick clouds and deep blackness.*
> *Suddenly, like dawn spreading across the mountains,*
> *a great and mighty army appears.*
> *Nothing like it has been seen before*
> *or will ever be seen again.*
> *3 Fire burns in front of them,*
> *and flames follow after them.*
> *Ahead of them the land lies as beautiful as the Garden of Eden.*
> *Behind them is nothing but desolation; not one thing escapes.*
> *4 They look like horses; they charge forward like warhorses.*
> *5 Look at them as they leap along the mountaintops.*
> *Listen to the noise they make—like the rumbling of chariots,*
> *like the roar of fire sweeping across a field of stubble,*
> *or like a mighty army moving into battle.*

6 Fear grips all the people;
every face grows pale with terror.
7 The attackers march like warriors and scale city walls like soldiers.
Straight forward they march, never breaking rank.
8 They never jostle each other; each moves in exactly the right position.
They break through defenses without missing a step.
9 They swarm over the city and run along its walls.
They enter all the houses, climbing like thieves through the windows.
10 The earth quakes as they advance, and the heavens tremble.
The sun and moon grow dark, and the stars no longer shine.
11 The Lord is at the head of the column.
He leads them with a shout.
This is his mighty army, and they follow his orders.
The day of the Lord is an awesome, terrible thing.
Who can possibly survive?"

We appeared seemingly out of nowhere, and began burning the NWO lies to the ground! We fight in this digital battle like warhorses and frighten the cabal to death! We follow the LORD'S directions, and are able to reach people by entering their houses through their social media accounts! The LORD is at the head of the column leading the battle!

11. What does it mean for the LORD to "open the graves of exile and cause you to rise again?"
    Ezekiel 37

    11 "Then he said to me, "Son of man, these bones represent the people of Israel. They are saying, 'We have become old, dry bones—all hope is gone. Our nation is finished.'
    12 Therefore, prophesy to them and say, 'This is what the Sovereign Lord says: O my people, I will open your graves of exile and cause you to rise again. Then I will bring you back to the land of Israel."

12. What land will He bring us back to? (Ezekiel 37:12)

I believe "open your graves of exile and cause you to rise" is describing humanity awakening so we regain our freedom from the satanic NWO that has ruled over us. "Bringing us back to the land of Israel" indicates that we will be sovereign individuals in our own land. We will know our identity as God's people, and we will rule and reign on earth.

13. How does this army fulfill Matthew 11:12?
    Matthew 11

12 "And from the time John the Baptist began preaching until now, the Kingdom of Heaven has been forcefully advancing, and violent people are attacking it."

We are advancing and taking back the narrative and the control one step at a time. We are peaceful, but we are forceful and we will not stop until we achieve victory!

14. What does the future hold for God's people, according to Revelation 5:10?

> Revelation 5
> *10 "And you have caused them to become*
> *a Kingdom of priests for our God.*
> *And they will reign on the earth."*

We will not be ruled over. We will have real self-rule and freedom for all of humanity. The righteous will run every organization.

15. What does it mean to return home to your own land, and to reign on the earth?

> Ezekiel 37
> *13 "When this happens, O my people, you will know that I am the Lord.*
> *14 I will put my Spirit in you, and you will live again and return home to your own land. Then you will know that I, the Lord, have spoken, and I have done what I said. Yes, the Lord has spoken!'"*

We will be sovereign individuals in our own land. We will know our identity as God's people, and we will rule on earth. We will no longer be oppressed and robbed and poisoned by the NWO.

16. Describe the glorious future for humanity when this battle is over! (see Joel 2:26-29)

> Joel 2
> *26 "Once again you will have all the food you want,*
> *and you will praise the Lord your God,*
> *who does these miracles for you.*
> *Never again will my people be disgraced.*
> *27 Then you will know that I am among my people Israel,*
> *that I am the Lord your God, and there is no other.*
> *Never again will my people be disgraced.*
> *28 "Then, after doing all those things,*
> *I will pour out my Spirit upon all people.*
> *Your sons and daughters will prophesy.*
> *Your old men will dream dreams,*
> *and your young men will see visions.*
> *29 In those days I will pour out my Spirit*

even on servants—men and women alike."

Everyone will have plenty. Everyone will know the LORD and honor Him. No one will be treated disgracefully. God's Spirit will fill every place!

6-SIX LIES WE WERE TOLD

"End Times and 1000 Years of Peace" Chapter 4

The Book of Revelation is hard enough to understand. But it's even harder to understand when we've been brainwashed with a tangled web of lies about End Times all our lives.

No worries… we will escape the End Times deception, one exposed lie at a time!
Let's get started!

ERROR # 1 EXPOSED -
Christians escape earth in the Rapture and don't fight Armageddon. NO!
It's Classic Brainwashing.
Take a truth. Twist the truth into a lie. Repeat it often, from every source, especially from trusted sources, like pastors, and people usually accept it. Classic.

This particular lie is called Rapture. And it worked like a charm, literally. Most Christians are not even trying to identify the Beast of Daniel and Revelation, because they have been misled to think the Beast will appear AFTER Christians escape in the Rapture. So they won't have to fight the Beast anyway. Good one, New World Order.

The verse they twist into deception, 1 Thessalonians 4:16-17, is not about escaping earth. It is about the Great Day when we will receive our incorruptible bodies!

We are not escaping earth. The LORD is going to reign on earth for 1,000 years, and we will reign with Him here, not on a cloud somewhere! The clouds symbolize power and authority, not escape!

Here's the passage that occurs after the 1,000 years of peace on earth, when we receive our incorruptible bodies.

> 1 Thessalonians 4
> *16 "For the Lord himself will come down from heaven with a commanding shout, with the voice of the archangel, and with the trumpet call of God. First, the believers who have died will rise from their graves.*

17 Then, together with them, we who are still alive and remain on the earth will be caught up in the clouds to meet the Lord in the air. Then we will be with the Lord forever."

1. Do you believe 1 Thessalonians 4:16-17 is about the great day when we will receive our incorruptible bodies? Or about believers escaping earth? Why?

When we will receive our incorruptible bodies. Because the verse say at that time the dead rise from their graves. All of humanity will become incorruptible at the same time, as verse 15 states, "We who are still living when the Lord returns will not meet him (new bodies) ahead of those who have died."

ERROR # 2 EXPOSED -
Pre-Trib, Mid-Trib, Post-Trib Rapture. NO!

This entire discussion is DIVERSION. They try to focus our attention on trying to figure out when the Rapture will occur...before the Tribulation, in the middle of the Tribulation, or after the Tribulation. Because Rapture is a DIVERSION too!

And there won't be a seven-year worldwide cataclysmic nuclear tribulation either. The whole discussion is one gigantic deception diversion. Most who "study" the Book of Revelation get so focused on whether the Rapture is Pre-Tribulation, Mid-Tribulation, or Post-Tribulation that they don't actually study the Book of Revelation! A DIVERSION inside a DIVERSION! Another good one, New World Order!

2. Why do you think most End Times studies focus the attention on the timeline placement of the Cataclysmic Tribulation and Rapture events? Maybe to make it appear that it is fact that there will be a worldwide cataclysmic Tribulation and a Rapture earth escape event? Thoughts?

Most of the modern End Times teachings consider the rapture to be an escape from earth that is a settled fact. The only question they discuss is WHEN this escape from earth will occur. Most don't ever consider that the "rapture" is AFTER the 1000 years of Christ's reign on earth, and after the Gog and Magog Battle, when satan and death are defeated and we receive our incorruptible bodies! That error was by NWO design to divert us from expecting to fight in the Battle of Armageddon.

ERROR # 3 EXPOSED -
One Left, One Taken verse is about Rapture. NO!

These two passages below SEEMINGLY contradict each other, logistically. But the riddle has been solved! The NWO infiltrated and told us the "One Taken" is the "Rapture." That was mass deception.

> Matthew 24
> *31 "And he will send out his angels with the mighty blast of a trumpet, and they will gather his chosen ones from all over the world—from the farthest ends of the earth and heaven."*

Compare to:

> Matthew 24
> *37 "When the Son of Man returns, it will be like it was in Noah's day.*
> *38 In those days before the flood, the people were enjoying banquets and parties and weddings right up to the time Noah entered his boat.*
> *39 People didn't realize what was going to happen until the flood came and swept them all away. That is the way it will be when the Son of Man comes.*
> *40 "Two men will be working together in the field; **one will be taken, the other left.***
> *41 Two women will be grinding flour at the mill; **one will be taken, the other left**."*

So, the questions are: Who is Taken? Who is Left? Who is Gathered? Good guys? Bad guys?

RIDDLE SOLVED!

Who is Gathered? The angels *gathered* the warriors from all over the world, to fight the enemy New World Order. Armageddon is an INFORMATION WAR. Our battlefield is the Internet. The angels do not have to MOVE us to a physical battlefield. Angels have gathered us from all over the world and we are fighting from our laptops and cell phones! (Of course, we certainly have White Hat military who will physically accomplish whatever is needed.)

When you think of "field," don't think about an area of land. Think about a "profession."

Who is "taken" from the "field?" All the criminals will be removed from their positions of authority and they will no longer be able to hurt the people, through "fields" of bad medicine, media, surveillance, GMOs, technology, etc.

Who is "left" in the "field?" Those who will use the "fields" of study for good, instead of evil, will be left to run the companies and organizations, media and education, etc. Which means health, wealth, and peace will permeate the entire world!

3. Who is left and who is taken in Matthew 24:37-41?

The righteous are left to inherit the earth and to rule. The NWO criminals are taken away to

judgment! They will be swept away!

ERROR # 4 EXPOSED -
The Battle of Armageddon is against the entire world of unbelievers! NO!
They have lead us to believe that when the LORD appears, there will be worldwide nuclear

devastation and calamity. That Armageddon fear-mongering propaganda is NOT TRUE! The truth is that Christ and His army of faithful patriots are fighting the Beast New World Order. Peace will settle over the earth because those who have been causing such turmoil and suffering and deception WILL BE STOPPED!

Did you catch that?! Armageddon is Good versus Evil. Patriots against the Beast – the New World Order – those creeps who worship Lucifer and get their power and wealth from doing evil. They are the ones who took the "Mark of Evil" (the Mark of the Beast)! They have done unspeakable crimes against humanity, and they will pay dearly. The LORD is saving us from their tyrannical, destructive rule! I repeat. The Battle of Armageddon is the Battle of Good vs Evil... not a worldwide annihilation of all of humanity! Now THAT'S Great News!
Everything we are doing to expose the corruption and lies is helping us win this battle of Armageddon! People are waking up and rising up to destroy the tyrants and their evil from the face of the earth.

4. What benefits would the NWO gain by causing Christians to believe Armageddon would be fought against non-Christians instead of being fought against the NWO criminal cabal?

The error that Armageddon is fought against non-Christians accomplishes several objectives for the NWO. It causes division and animosity between people groups, which helps to stoke war. Sadly, many people believe God hates non-Christians, so it is ok to hate them too, just because of their beliefs. It also keeps Christians from identifying and fighting our real enemy, the NWO satanic criminal cabal.

ERROR # 5 EXPOSED -
Armageddon is a Physical War in the Jezreel Valley between a "Nation from the North" and Iraq. NO!
All of the Bible has come alive since the Great Awakening began, especially since realizing the New World Order is the Beast of Revelation. So I'm really not intending to be disrespectful to people who explain these passages without this information/revelation. But I am trying to shed light on these passages in view of what we have learned recently. No doubt, the deceivers have tried to send us on a wild goose chase. And those who are deceived, unwittingly pass on the deception....and so on and on and on.

First off, we know that Armageddon is NOT a physical battle.
We are fighting a spiritual war of Good versus Evil.
We are fighting a "Worldwide Mafia Cabal of satanists."

Armageddon is NOT a war between nations, as we typically think of nations. So when we read prophecies from books like Jeremiah and Isaiah, loaded with symbolism, we have to take this into account. Babylon is the New World Order. The Army from the North is the worldwide Patriots, which is the same army of Revelation 14 and Joel 2. When you read Jeremiah 50 about the "Nation from the North" in this light, you know it's talking about the Patriots destroying Babylon/NWO.

> Jeremiah 50
> 3 "For a nation will attack her from the north and bring such destruction that no one will live there again. Everything will be gone; both people and animals will flee."
>
> 9 "For I am raising up an army
> of great nations from the north.
> They will join forces to attack Babylon,
> and she will be captured.
> The enemies' arrows will go straight to the mark;
> they will not miss!"

Just read the destruction we are wreaking on the New World Order, and you know this passage is talking about the Patriots.

> Jeremiah 50
> 14 "Yes, prepare to attack Babylon,
> all you surrounding nations.
> Let your archers shoot at her; spare no arrows.
> For she has sinned against the Lord.
> 15 Shout war cries against her from every side.
> Look! She surrenders!
> Her walls have fallen.
> It is the Lord's vengeance,
> so take vengeance on her.
> Do to her as she has done to others!"

That's **us** shooting Truth Arrows! Sparing no arrows! And **we** are "doing unto her as she has done"! Notice it says, "her walls have fallen," as in "Babylon (NWO) is Fallen!"

5. What benefits would the NWO gain by causing us to believe Armageddon would be fought in a physical battlefield, rather than a digital battle between good and evil?

**Most Christians are expecting Armageddon to be a tactile battle in the Jezreel Valley. Of course, the NWO wouldn't allow that to happen. Most Christians can't imagine that Armageddon is actually fought on the digital battlefield, destroying the evil NWO on social media. So most are sleeping right through Armageddon.**

ERROR # 6 EXPOSED -
The Mark of the Beast is a Physical Mark/Chip required on all of humanity! NO!

This deception caused many to believe that God was going to destroy every man, woman, and child who took a Mark of the Beast tattoo or a chip in order to survive and save their families. Can you imagine? The LORD would never punish people for doing that! The Mark of the Beast has nothing to do with tattoos or chips at all! That is NOT the Mark of the Beast.

The Mark of the Beast is the Mark of PURE EVIL – participating in satanic rituals and acting under the influence of demons. This is the "mark" that the New World Order minions have taken in order to gain wealth and privilege. They have been willing to do anything and say anything so they could be part of this "elite" club. These people are SICK!

> Revelation 13
>
> 16 "He required everyone—small and great, rich and poor, free and slave—to be given a mark on the right hand or on the forehead.
>
> 17 And no one could buy or sell anything without that mark, which was either the name of the beast or the number representing his name."

Here is the explanation of this mis-taught passage: In order to benefit financially, and receive positions and power, all kinds of people, from all over the world, have joined this evil secret society. It doesn't say every man, woman, and child, but all KINDS of people. Think about it. Have most people been truly free to buy and sell? To gain true wealth? NO! The stock market is rigged. The education system is rigged. The jobs are rigged. The prices make it almost impossible to survive without going into debt slavery!

Except for a few, only the minions of the New World Order cabal have truly had the power to buy and sell, and become rich and powerful, while the rest of us have been left outside, to struggle and lose our health and wealth.

Angry yet?

We have had tribulation on a mass worldwide scale... from Venezuela to North Korea to China to Africa to the financial and health and cultural devastation in America and all around the world. The world almost collapsed into complete slavery, but thank the LORD we are in the GREAT AWAKENING. The whole world is waking up and casting out these evil tyrants!

If you have learned of the evils of human trafficking that are done by the New World Order, and how people have joined in league with them to enslave humanity, they perfectly fit the description of the Beast of Revelation. These people are literally demon-possessed and have taken on the Mark of the Beast by committing unspeakable rituals. They have rigged everything so they are the only ones who have been able to gain true wealth, while we became poorer and enslaved. That is what the Mark of the Beast is...not the ridiculous and disrespectful notion that the LORD will destroy people who take a chip to save their families! The truth is that those who have done horrifying satanic rituals WILL be destroyed! This is the truth. We are all coming out of the deception that has been force-fed to the masses. Finally!

Those of us who studied the Revelation, were force-fed the popular explanations, which left us scratching our heads because none of them made sense, or jibed with Scripture. But now we realize it was filled with deception to hide the Beast/New World Order!

6. What benefits would the NWO gain by causing us to believe the Mark of the Beast is a chip/jab rather than the mark of taking in and being led by demonic entities?

The last thing the cabal wants us to realize is that they have taken the Mark of the Beast by taking in demons and joining them to destroy humanity. By convincing many Christians to believe the Mark is a chip or a jab, they divert attention from their crimes and their level of depravity. Many Christians are scared they have taken the Mark of the Beast, and have no idea what the Mark REALLY is.

7. Do you think the controlled seminaries have lead us into these End Times errors? Who do you think funds and controls most seminaries?

Yes. The Church and the seminaries are highly infiltrated by the cabal by Soros and the NWO. They prevent those who think and speak for themselves from speaking End Times truth in the Church, and exposing the cabal. They intentionally misled us about End Times.

7-SIX MORE LIES WE WERE TOLD

"End Times and 1000 Years of Peace" Chapter 4

Let's keep blasting through the End Times deceptions!

ERROR # 7 EXPOSED -
The third temple MUST be built before the Battle of Armageddon. NO!
And they also say that the "Anti-Christ must go and sit in that temple and proclaim himself as god." (from 2 Thessalonians 2:4) Well, my response is, "the Beast would never allow a third temple to be built!" Because that would prompt Christians to wake up and fight the Beast! So long as the temple is never built, there can be no Anti-Christ to go sit inside it! And that prevents Christians from ever identifying the Beast of Revelation! And the New World Order Beast can continue destroying the world all day, every day! Good one, New World Order.

Get it? Imagine you're a thief. You tell people that they will know the bank has been robbed when the front door is broken into. But you rob the bank going through the back door! The people never catch on! And you laugh, and Laugh, and LAUGH!

"Sitting in the temple and proclaiming himself to be god" is symbolism. It means that the Anti-Christ/New World Order/Beast acts like they are god on earth. Telling everyone what to do. Demanding absolute obedience. Financially enslaving. Removing prayer. Forcing Anti-God education down our throats. Flooding the airwaves with lies and filth against God. No doubt this describes the NWO perfectly! Catching on to their little game?

The Beast/New World Order works perfectly, so long as the masses never put two and two together! Once we do, their little evil scheme comes unglued! And THAT, my friends, is what has happened! The entire WORLD has awakened to our true enemy...the New World Order Bloodline Luciferian Globalist International Bankers. Everyone except the Church at large. Shockingly, most Christians are still sitting on their hands, waiting for the third temple. If believers are waiting for their church leaders to identify the Beast, and Armageddon, and the Great Awakening, they are likely in for a long wait.

1. Why will the New World Order never all the Third Temple to be built?

To keep Christians asleep. They teach that only after the building of a physical third temple, will the AntiChrist be reveald, and Tribulation and Armageddon are after that. The truth is that the third temple is in us! We are the house the AntiChrist wants to sit in! WE SAY NO!

ERROR # 8 EXPOSED -
The Tribulation hasn't happened yet. NO!

I shake my head whenever I hear someone say "The Tribulation" hasn't happened yet. Really? Are you kidding me? The world is in ruins! As President Trump says, this is our last chance to save our Country. And even the world. THE LORD WILL PREVENT THE WORLD FROM BEING DESTROYED IN A NUCLEAR HOLOCAUST LIKE THE MODERN END TIMES TEACHING TOLD US WOULD HAPPEN.

China is a Communist Slave State.
Venezuelans are literally starving under Maduro's brutal dictatorship.
North Koreans have been under a brutal regime directly by the New World Order.
Europe is in shambles since the EU took over, and the migrants have flooded in.
Mexico is in utter ruin being tyrannized by drug lords.
Africa for years has continually had its assets stolen, not to mention the prolific evil of organ harvesting.
Until recently, Saudi Arabia was the head of worldwide human trafficking.
Most of the Middle East has held the people in untold oppression.
And America…oh dear, America. Under silent assault from every direction.
I didn't even mention the continual massive wars and all the deadly diseases. So yes, the world has had tribulation upon tribulation. I hope I never hear another person say in my lifetime that there has been no tribulation. Because it still rings in my ears and I'm shaking my head at the incredible deception!

2. Describe the Modern End Times teaching about what happens during Tribulation.

The Modern End Times teaching is that Christians escape earth and then the nuclear holocaust tribulation starts, and non-Christians suffer untold misery and death worldwide.

3. Describe the Tribulation humanity has experienced.

We have all been increasing oppressed worldwide under the NWO tyranny, through continual wars, financial hardship, widespread planned chronic illness, and outrageous dystopic public policy to destroy our culture, remove our rights of speech and fair elections, and force us under communist totalitarianism. The rise in mental illness and plummeting birth rates show definitively that humanity is at the end of the time of Tribulation and must defeat the NWO once and for all.

ERROR # 9 EXPOSED -
There will be seven years of Worldwide Nuclear Cataclysmic Tribulation. NO!
The New World Order minions infiltrated the seminaries and spread this error throughout the Church and entertainment. They said there is a remaining week in Daniel's prophecy that equates to seven years of worldwide catastrophic tribulation.
Most don't know that this widespread teaching comes from a very complex passage tucked in Daniel Chapter 9. We SHOULD NEVER build a super-structure of "End Times" or any other theology on an obscure passage filled with complicated symbolism. But that is EXACTLY what they did. See Chapter 5 "Tribulation Fake News", explaining Daniel 9.

4. What is the danger of using a very complex passage with complicated symbolism as the basis for End Times teaching? Could it be used to trick and manipulate the masses?

It is not wise to build doctrine on a single obsure and complex passage of prophecy. This prophecy has been misused to trick the masses into expecting the AntiChrist to enter the third temple in Jerusalem, and to rule the earth from there. Most never even consider that the AntiChrist is the NWO who is oppressing them!

ERROR # 10 EXPOSED -
The Anti-Christ Man of Lawlessness has not come yet. NO!
How would anyone recognize the Anti-Christ? Who gets to proclaim a person as the Anti-Christ? Check out this passage and then we can talk about it.

> 2 Thessalonians 2
> 3 *"Don't be fooled by what they say. For that day will not come until there is a great rebellion against God and the man of lawlessness (AntiChrist) is <u>revealed</u>—the one who brings destruction.*
> 4 <u>*He will exalt himself and defy everything that people call god and every object of worship. He will even sit in the temple of God, claiming that he himself is God.*</u>
> 5 *Don't you remember that I told you about all this when I was with you?*
> 6 *And you know what is holding him back, for he can be revealed only when his time comes.*
> 7 *For this lawlessness is already at work secretly, and it will remain secret until the one who is holding it back steps out of the way.*
> 8 *Then the man of lawlessness will be revealed, but the Lord Jesus will slay him with the breath of his mouth and destroy him by the splendor of his coming.*

9 This man will come to do the work of Satan with counterfeit power and signs and miracles.

10 He will use every kind of evil deception to fool those on their way to destruction, because they refuse to love and accept the truth that would save them.

11 So God will cause them to be greatly deceived, and they will believe these lies.

12 Then they will be condemned for enjoying evil rather than believing the truth."

So in this passage, the Lawless One is the Son of Destruction, aka Son of Perdition, aka Anti-Christ. *He will be accompanied by the working of satan, with every kind of power, sign, and false wonder, and with every wicked deception.*

Who does that sound like to you? All together now!
The New World Order Globalist Bloodlines!
THEY ARE THE ANTICHRIST!

We are not waiting for the AntiChrist to go sit in a temple. The Beast would never allow that! The Lawless One has been revealed. That is what the Great Awakening is all about. We know who our enemy is now. And that enemy is being destroyed! What a GREAT DAY!

The GREAT DECEPTION is referring to those who worked with the Beast (NWO) being deceived into doing evil and spreading lies and working injustice, in order to be rich and powerful. That is the GREAT DECEPTION. And they made a very, very bad choice. These past few years have given them one last opportunity to come out of this cabal before it is too late.

5. Do you believe the AntiChrist has been revealed? Do you believe the New World Order Criminal Cabal is the AntiChrist? Why or why not?

I do believe the NWO has been revealed as the AntiChrist. I do not believe the AntiChrist is an individual but a highly organized group that works together to rule over humanity. I believe they have brought destruction on the earth, and they expect us to obey them as if they are God.

ERROR #11 EXPOSED -
The Name Jew Always Describes the Physical Lineage of Judah. The Name Israel Always Describes the Physical Lineage of Jacob. NO!
When you read the word Israelite or Jew or Hebrew, sometimes the context is about the physical lineage, but many times it is talking about "God's family" in general. Many believers are actually in the physical line of the Lost Tribes of Israel! Other believers have been adopted into God's family. Either way, believers from every nation are what the Bible calls **True Israelites**...**True Jews**...**True Hebrews**...the **True Family of God**. This is very important. The enemy has used the confusion about the word Jew and Israelite to cause unbelievable confusion.

Romans 2

28 "For you are not a true Jew just because you were born of Jewish parents or because you have gone through the ceremony of circumcision.

*29 No, **a true Jew is one whose heart is right with God**. And true circumcision is not merely obeying the letter of the law; rather, **it is a change of heart produced by the Spirit**. And a person with a changed heart seeks praise from God, not from people."*

Galatians 3

28 "There is no longer Jew or Gentile, slave or free, male and female. For you are all one in Christ Jesus.

29 And now that you belong to Christ, you are the true children of Abraham. You are his heirs, and God's promise to Abraham belongs to you."

The LORD counts a Jew as someone who follows Him from their heart. Sadly there are many who claim to be Jews who do not follow the LORD, and are not physical Jews either, but have hijacked the name Jew for evil purposes.

6. How did Paul describe a true Jew in the passages above?

__Being a true Jew is not about ethnicity, but about faith. According to God's Word, those who__

__follow God are true children of Abraham and heirs of God's promises.__

7. How does the world describe a true Jew?

__Only those who say they are of Jewish ethnicity or who follow Judaism or other offshoots of the__

__Jewish religion.__

8. What benefit is it to the New World Order to hijack the name Jew? As in Revelation 2:9 & 3:9. Explain.

__They can proclaim themselves God's chosen people, and take the land God promised to Abraham.__

__They can use the name to convince the world to support them no matter what they do, and that__

__they cannot be questioned about their actions. Revelation 2:9 and 3:9 both warn us that there__

__are some who say they are Jews but are not, and are actually the synagogue of satan.__

ERROR # 12 EXPOSED -
"Fleeing into the mountains" verse is for future Tribulation. NO!

Matthew 24

15 "The day is coming when you will see what Daniel the prophet spoke about—the sacrilegious object that causes desecration standing in the Holy Place."(Reader, pay attention!) 16 "Then those in Judea must flee to the hills. 17 A person out on the deck of a roof must not go down into the house to pack. 18 A person out in the field must not return even to get a coat. 19 How terrible it will be for pregnant women and for nursing mothers in those days. 20 And pray that your flight will not be in winter or on the Sabbath."

Jesus asked His disciples what they thought about those buildings - namely the Temple in Jerusalem. He warned them of those buildings' coming destruction. And it happened just as our LORD Jesus said it would. There was horrifying abomination of desolation committed in the temple, straight from the pits of hell. Just as we have learned about happening in tunnels underground. The Romans destroyed Jerusalem in A.D. 70. They pushed every stone off the temple mount to the ground far below. Not one stone was left on another. That is where the stones lay to this day. THAT is what Jesus was talking about in this passage. This event has already happened. This passage is NOT about a future event.

9. The New World Order has instilled great fear about the Tribulation, in order to manipulate believers. Most expect to "flee to the mountains." What is this passage really talking about?

This passage is where Jesus was warning the disciples about the time when the Romans would destroy Jerusalem, and that the people would survive only if they fled to the mountains. The Romans sacked Jerusalem in A.D. 70, just as our LORD Jesus predicted.

Of course, there are more errors the NWO used to instill fear and manipulate Christians. But these twelve errors gives you a good start in shaking free from the matrix of End Times Lies. Now you're ready to dive deeper into the "Tribulation Fake News."

8-TRIBULATION FAKE NEWS

"End Times and 1000 Years of Peace" Chapter 5

What is the #1 **Fake News** about End Times?
The seven-year **Nuclear Cataclysmic Tribulation Destruction of Humanity**.

The End Times so-called scholars and Hollywood have just about convinced everyone that the world will experience a worldwide nuclear holocaust destruction.

1. Why might the cabal want us to believe the world will be destroyed in a worldwide nuclear holocaust?

They do not want us to envision the Millennial Kingdom of Christ on earth. They want us to envision God's indiscriminate destruction of humanity, as if God hates humanity. Of course that does not reconcile with Scripture or that our LORD Jesus died for humanity.

2. Give one of the LORD'S promises so we know the world will NOT be destroyed with a nuclear holocaust. (provide Scripture reference)

"Nothing will hurt or destroy in all my holy mountain, for as the waters fill the sea, so the earth will be filled with people who know the Lord." Isaiah 11:9

Daniel 9:24 is the Scripture many point to regarding a seven-year tribulation and destruction of humanity.
Want to know what this passage is REALLY about?
This prophecy is about 70 "weeks" which the LORD told us would be determined for Christ to fulfill His promise to **save** humanity!

> Daniel 9:24 (NKJV)
> *24 "Seventy weeks are determined*
> *For your people and for your holy city,*
> *To finish the transgression,*

To make an end of sins,
To make reconciliation for iniquity,
To bring in everlasting righteousness,
To seal up vision and prophecy,
And to anoint the Most Holy."

3. Write down the promises in Daniel 9 here:

Put an "X" beside the promises that have been completely fulfilled.

To finish the transgression, W

To make an end of sins, W

To make reconciliation for iniquity, W

To bring in everlasting righteousness, W

To seal up vision and prophecy, W

And to anoint the Most Holy. X

Put a "W" for WAITING for the promises we are still awaiting fulfillment.
Discuss.

Respectfully, at the cross our LORD Jesus accomplished salvation for humanity, but many of the promises are still in process. Transgressions and sins are still ongoing. Iniquity has been reconciled ultimately, but each of us work out our reconciliation daily with the LORD. Everlasting righteousness has not be completed and neither has the vision and prophecy. But the Most Holy has been anointed with the blood of Christ. If you would like to lear about this, search "03-31-21 The Ark of the Covenant was Found." These promises were fulfilled at the cross, but not completed fully until heaven on earth, in my opinion.

4. Seventy normal weeks would be how many days? ***490 days***
These are clearly not typical seven-day weeks.

5. Where should we find the meaning of the Biblical weeks? ***In the Bible!***

This is the Festival of WEEKS the LORD told us to celebrate perpetually. It is found in Leviticus 23:10-22 and Leviticus 25:1-17. This is very important in order to understand the weeks in Daniel 9. Read these passages to become familiar with the Annual Festival, the 7th-year Sabbath, and the 50th Year Jubilee.

Leviticus 23

Annual Festival of Weeks

10 "Give the following instructions to the people of Israel. When you enter the land I am giving you and you harvest its first crops, bring the priest a bundle of grain (omer) from the first cutting (firstfruits) of your grain harvest.

11 On the day after the Sabbath, the priest will lift it (the omer) up before the Lord so it may be accepted on your behalf.

12 On that same day you must sacrifice a one-year-old male lamb with no defects as a burnt offering to the Lord.

13 With it you must present a grain offering consisting of four quarts of choice flour moistened with olive oil. It will be a special gift, a pleasing aroma to the Lord. You must also offer one quart of wine as a liquid offering.

14 Do not eat any bread or roasted grain or fresh kernels on that day until you bring this offering to your God. This is a permanent law for you, and it must be observed from generation to generation wherever you live.

*15 "From the day after the Sabbath—the day you bring the bundle of grain (omer) to be lifted up as a special offering—count off **seven full weeks**.*

*16 Keep counting until the day after the **seventh Sabbath (week)**, fifty days later. Then present an offering of new grain to the Lord.*

17 From wherever you live, bring two loaves of bread to be lifted up before the Lord as a special offering. Make these loaves from four quarts of choice flour, and bake them with yeast. They will be an offering (firstfruits) to the Lord from the first of your crops.

18 Along with the bread, present seven one-year-old male lambs with no defects, one young bull, and two rams as burnt offerings to the Lord. These burnt offerings, together with the grain offerings and liquid offerings, will be a special gift, a pleasing aroma to the Lord.

19 Then you must offer one male goat as a sin offering and two one-year-old male lambs as a peace offering.

20 "The priest will lift up the two lambs as a special offering to the Lord, together with the loaves representing the first of your crops. These offerings, which are holy to the Lord, belong to the priests.

21 That same day will be proclaimed an official day for holy assembly, a day on which you do no ordinary work. This is a permanent law for you, and it must be observed from generation to generation wherever you live.

22 "When you harvest the crops of your land, do not harvest the grain along the edges of your fields, and do not pick up what the harvesters drop. Leave it for the poor and the foreigners living among you. I am the Lord your God."

Leviticus 25

Seven-Year Sabbath Rest (Vacation)

1 "While Moses was on Mount Sinai, the Lord said to him,

2 "Give the following instructions to the people of Israel. When you have entered the land I am giving you, the land itself must observe a Sabbath rest before the Lord every seventh year.

3 For six years you may plant your fields and prune your vineyards and harvest your crops,

*4 but during the **seventh year the land must have a Sabbath year of complete rest**. It is the Lord's Sabbath. Do not plant your fields or prune your vineyards during that year.*

5 And don't store away the crops that grow on their own or gather the grapes from your unpruned vines. The land must have a year of complete rest.

6 But you may eat whatever the land produces on its own during its Sabbath. This applies to you, your male and female servants, your hired workers, and the temporary residents who live with you.

7 Your livestock and the wild animals in your land will also be allowed to eat what the land produces."

YEAR OF JUBILEE - Year 50 – Debts Canceled and Captives Freed!

8 "In addition, you must count off seven Sabbath years, seven sets of seven years, adding up to forty-nine years in all.

9 Then on the Day of Atonement in the fiftieth year, blow the ram's horn loud and long throughout the land.

*10 **Set this year apart as holy, a time to proclaim freedom throughout the land for all who live there. It will be a jubilee year for you, when each of you may return to the land that belonged to your ancestors and return to your own clan**.*

11 This fiftieth year will be a jubilee for you. During that year you must not plant your fields or store away any of the crops that grow on their own, and don't gather the grapes from your unpruned vines.

12 It will be a jubilee year for you, and you must keep it holy. But you may eat whatever the land produces on its own.

13 In the Year of Jubilee each of you may return to the land that belonged to your ancestors.

14 "When you make an agreement with your neighbor to buy or sell property, you must not take advantage of each other.

15 When you buy land from your neighbor, the price you pay must be based on the number of years since the last jubilee. The seller must set the price by taking into account the number of years remaining until the next Year of Jubilee.

16 The more years until the next jubilee, the higher the price; the fewer years, the lower the price. After all, the person selling the land is actually selling you a certain number of harvests.

17 Show your fear of God by not taking advantage of each other. I am the Lord your God."

6. Each year, the Festival of Weeks celebration is a practice for the seventh year Sabbath rest, and the fiftieth year Jubilee. Do you think weeks in Daniel could be referring to the Festival of Weeks?

Yes! That's exactly what Daniel was referring to!

7. This is how the Annual Festival of Weeks is celebrated.
We celebrate the Spring Harvest by counting the **OMER** (AKA sheaves of grain). (see Leviticus 23:15) We are to count one per day over seven weeks (which is 49 days). The seven-week period is also called a "7."

8. We begin counting the grain on Resurrection Day (Easter).
That day is known in the Old Testament as the Festival of **WEEKS.**
(see Leviticus 23:10)

> Leviticus 23
> 10 *"Give the following instructions to the people of Israel. When you enter the land I am giving you and you harvest its first crops, bring the priest a bundle of grain (omer) from the first cutting (firstfruits) of your grain harvest."*

9. We add an omer grain to the bundle every day. This seven-week period is called the Festival of **Weeks**, also known as the Counting of the **Omer.**

10. The 50th Day of the Festival of Weeks is called **Pentecost.**

This was the day when the LORD sent the Holy Spirit to His disciples whom He told to wait in Jerusalem until they received power from on high. They would need the power of the Holy Spirit to preach the Gospel, speak in other languages, and to do various miracles. (see Acts 2)

11. What is proclaimed on the Day of Atonement in the 50th year, according to Leviticus 25:10? Think of a GOLDEN ANNIVERSARY PROCLAMATION!

> Leviticus 25
> 10 *"Set this year apart as holy, a time to proclaim freedom throughout the land for all who live there. It will be a jubilee year for you, when each of you may return to the land that belonged to your ancestors and return to your own clan."*

Freedom is proclaimed! The Year of Jubilee is celebrated with debts canceled and captives freed!

12. Summarize what happens during the Jubilee Year, according to Leviticus 25:8-17.

One year every 50 years everyone takes a vacation! Everyone's debts are canceled and the captives are freed! During the Jubilee year even the land rests. Everyone takes a break from the unending hustle, and actually relaxes. Everyone lives off what had been acquired in the prior years. Similar to how Joseph stored up grain for the people to have during the famine.

13. List some reasons the LORD commanded Jubilee every 50 years.
(Think of the condition humanity comes to, if Jubilee is not followed every 50 years.)

That means no one is in perpetual debt and slavery!

That means a small group cannot confiscate all the assets and leave the rest of humanity broke.

14. Has Jubilee been kept according to God's Word? **_NO._**

15. Was Jubilee ever kept since Daniel's "70 weeks" prophecy? If so, when and by whom?
(See Nehemiah 5:10-12)

> Nehemiah 5
> *10 "I myself, as well as my brothers and my workers, have been lending the people money and grain, but now let us stop this business of charging interest.*
> *11 You must restore their fields, vineyards, olive groves, and homes to them this very day. And repay the interest you charged when you lent them money, grain, new wine, and olive oil."*
> *12 They replied, "We will give back everything and demand nothing more from the people. We will do as you say." Then I called the priests and made the nobles and officials swear to do what they had promised."*

Nehemiah and Ezra kept the Jubilee during their time of authority, when they brought the

Israelites back to Jerusalem from being captive in Babylon.

16. Was Jubilee kept during the rest of the "70 weeks?"

Sadly, no. I have not found any historical evidence of Jubilee since the time of Nehemiah.

Ready to finally know what this has to do with the remaining seven weeks in Daniel 9:24-27?
It's a HUGE CLUE!

> Daniel 9
> *24 "Seventy **weeks (7's)** are determined*
> *upon thy people and upon thy holy city...*
> *27"from the going forth of the commandment to restore and to build Jerusalem unto Messiah the Prince shall be **seven weeks (7's), and threescore and two weeks(7's)."***

Now, let's do some simple math. (NOTE - 1 score = 20, so threescore = 60)

      7 "weeks" (seven 7-year periods)
60 and 2 "weeks" = _62 "weeks"_ (62 7-year periods)

TOTAL WEEKS   = 69 "weeks"

NOTICE WE ARE MISSING ONE "WEEK." (One seven-year period)

But why did the LORD separate seven "weeks" from 62 "weeks."

BECAUSE THE FIRST 7 "WEEKS" WAS THE ONLY TIME JUBILEE WAS KEPT!

Jubilee was never kept during the remaining 62 weeks that culminated with Christ entering Jerusalem. Rather than letting our Lord Jesus celebrate Jubilee by canceling debts and setting the captives free, He was "cut off" as He suffered for our sins on the cross.

THAT'S THE ANSWER!

The 70 Weeks in Daniel 9 are about keeping JUBILEE! Of course the controllers don't want us to know that!!! See on this chart below from page 43 of "End Times and 1000 Years of Peace" showing that Daniel's prophecy is all about Jubilees! The first **seven weeks** on the chart is the first Jubilee held in the land of Israel, when the people returned from Babylonian captivity. (Nehemiah 5)

But notice Jubilee was never kept during the following Jubilee cycles. Sadly, notice that Christ was cut off before the 10th Jubilee celebration. Refer to the illustration on the next page.

7 "WEEKS"   (1 7-yr period)   **70 "WEEKS"**

63 "WEEKS" (9 7-yr periods)	(10 JUBILEES)	CELEBRATE?	EST. YEAR
		Edict to Rebuild	~467 BC
Edict Marker = 7 "weeks"	Jubilee 1	Nehemiah's Jubilee	~417 BC
*1st "7" = 7 "weeks"	Jubilee 2	NO JUBILEE	367 BC
+ 2nd "7"= 14 "weeks"	Jubilee 3	NO JUBILEE	317 BC
+ 3rd "7" = 21 "weeks"	Jubilee 4	NO JUBILEE	267 BC
+ 4th "7" = 28 "weeks"	Jubilee 5	NO JUBILEE	217 BC
+ 5th "7" = 35 "weeks"	Jubilee 6	NO JUBILEE	167 BC
+ 6th "7" = 42 "weeks"	Jubilee 7	NO JUBILEE	117 BC
+ 7th "7" = 49 "weeks"	Jubilee 8	NO JUBILEE	67 BC
+ 8th "7" = 56 "weeks"	Jubilee 9	NO JUBILEE	17 BC
+ 9th "7" = 63 "weeks"	Jubilee 10	JESUS CUT OFF	33 AD

70 WEEKS = 10 JUBILEES!!!

17. What did faithful Nehemiah do for the people who returned from Babylon to Jerusalem, at the completion of the 7th seven-year period? (Nehemiah 5 - Think debts, land, prison etc.)

__Nehemiah and Ezra kept the Jubilee. They made sure there was no oppression in Israel. They made the people pay back any interest they have charged, and restore the fields or homes they had taken! Imagine that! Jubilee will happen!__

18. What did the unfaithful leaders do for the next nine Jubilees?

__The unfaithful leaders made up every excuse imagineable as to why they couldn't keep the Jubilee. The people eventually gave up trying to have those in authority celebrate Jubilee.__

We have decoded the hardest part of Daniel's prophecy!
Daniel was giving us clues about the Jubilee Emancipation Celebration!
The LORD knew the evil leaders would never celebrate Jubilee because they put the people in debt slavery on purpose!

So let's re-read the rest of the prophecy in Daniel 9.
(I've added some notes in brackets to help clarify – to help unlearn the lies.)

> Daniel 9
> 24 "*Seventy weeks* **(seven-year periods)** *are determined upon thy people and upon thy holy city, to finish the transgression, and to make an end of sins, and to make reconciliation for iniquity, and to bring in everlasting righteousness, and to seal up the vision and prophecy, and to anoint the most Holy.*
> 25 *Know therefore and understand, that from the going forth of the commandment to restored to build Jerusalem* **(Nehemiah)** *unto the Messiah the Prince* **(Jesus)** *shall be* ***seven weeks, and threescore and two weeks*** **(69 weeks)**: *the street shall be built again, and the wall, even in troublous times.* **(see also Nehemiah 3)**
> 26 *And after* ***threescore and two weeks*** *shall Messiah be cut off, but not for himself:* **(Christ went to the cross for our sins, not for His own sins)**
> *and the people of the prince* **(of darkness)** *that shall come shall destroy the city* **(God's people)** *and the sanctuary* **(God's people)***; and the end thereof shall be with a flood,*
> **(of evil done by the evildoers)** *and unto the end of the war* **(Armageddon)** *desolations* **(on earth)** *are determined.*
> (NKJV for clarity)
> 27 *And he* **(Christ)** *shall confirm the* **(70 week)** *covenant promise with many for* ***one week:*** **(remaining 7-year period)** *and in the midst of the week he shall cause the*

(demonic) *sacrifice and the oblation to cease, and for the* (worldwide) *overspreading of abominations* (on humanity) *he* (Christ) *shall make it* (the NWO) *desolate, even until the consummation* (of Armageddon), *and that determined* (punishment) *shall be poured upon the desolate* (evildoers)."

19. Let's look at the week 62. What does Daniel 9:26a say will happen to the Messiah after 62 "weeks?"

__Messiah be cut off, but not for himself__

20. Based on the Biblical Festivals, what were the religious leaders afraid Jesus was going to do for the people when He entered Jerusalem, if he was not cut off from doing so?

__They were afraid Jesus would institute the Jubilee and force them to return all the assets they__

__had taken from the people.__

21. Now we know Jesus is planning to institute Jubilee (Gesara) upon His return and taking power. We also know the remaining 7-year period is tribulation, as in the Awakening and the Digital Battle we are fighting against the NWO, raither than a nuclear holocaust.

So now let's dig into Daniel 9:27.

The enemy deceived humanity, building an entire narrative of fear on Daniel 9:27. Many interpretations say this verse is all about the AntiChrist. The word covenant was changed to treaty, and we were told the AntiChrist would sign a peace treaty. That made the world afraid of peace treaties! How deceitful is that?!

Let's fill in the blanks the accurate way, with our Lord Jesus being the one who confirms the covenant promise to rescue humanity, and to destroy the evildoers!

> A - *"And he (* *__Jesus Christ__* *) shall confirm the covenant with many for one week:*
>
> B - *and in the midst of the week* **he shall cause the sacrifice and the oblation to cease,**
>
> *(what evil sacrifice and oblation?* *__The NWO Baal sacrifices__* *)*
>
> C - *and for the overspreading of abominations he (* *__Christ__* *) shall make it (* *__the NWO__* *) desolate, even until the consummation, and that determined (* *__Judgment__* *) shall be poured upon the desolate."*
>
> (see Daniel 9:27 above)

Compare the False and True interpretations of Daniel 9:27

FALSE INTERPRETATION   **TRUE INTERPRETATION**

22. (A above) - Who will "confirm the covenant promise with many for one week?"

> *__AntiChrist__*   *__Our LORD Jesus Christ__*

FALSE INTERPRETATION   **TRUE INTERPRETATION**

23. (B above) What sacrifice and oblation will be stopped?

**Worship of the LORD** _**NWO Baal Sacrifices**_

(Hint - What sacrifices have occurred underneath our feet, without our knowledge?)

FALSE INTERPRETATION **TRUE INTERPRETATION**

24. (C Above) Who will be made desolate?

**Humanity** _**NWO AntiChrist**_

Our LORD is going to fulfill His covenant promises in Daniel 9:27 to destroy those who have caused horrifying devastation on the earth. Instead of thinking of worldwide nuclear war and tribulation on humanity, think of worldwide devastation on the New World Order Beast AntiChrist!

THAT is what they didn't want us to know!

THAT is why they created this false interpretation of Daniel 9:24-27!

Now you know why they deceived us about the "sacrifices and oblation," because they never wanted that truth about child sacrifice to come out!

Now you know why they lied to us about seven years of tribulation/destruction of humanity.

The NWO wanted us to think the defeat and destruction of humanity was inevitable.

They wanted us to think of ESCAPE…instead of FIGHTING ARMAGEDDON and defeating the New World Order!

YAHOOOOOO!!!!!

MYSTERY SOLVED!

EXTRA THOUGHTS

This is just speculation…It sure would be great if the LORD gave us an alarm clock.

Well…it just so happens He did! It's called the Mazzaroth – which is all the stars the LORD put in the heavens for _"signs, seasons, days and years,"_ according to Genesis 1:14.

This alarm went off September 23, 2017, based on Revelation 12:1-2. This beautiful sign is called the _"woman in labor"_ 18 times in the Old Testament too!

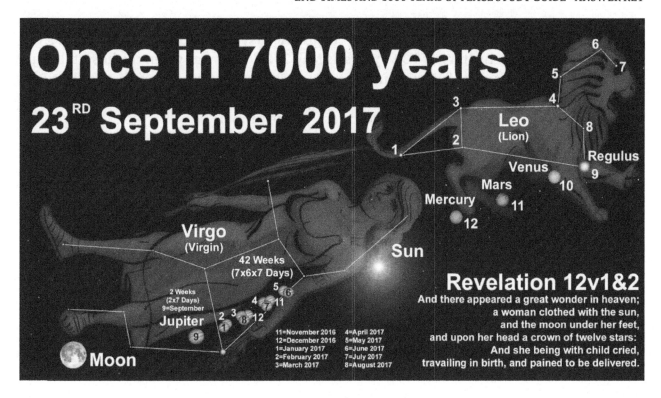

No doubt we have had worldwide battle since this sign occurred! Actually, the battle between good and evil has been going on for thousands of years...but this alarm clock marked the beginning of the final battle of Armageddon against the New World Order Beast of Revelation, also known as the AntiChrist. This was our wake-up call to discover who our enemy was and to start fighting them!

25. If this is the alarm that woke up humanity, the next question is...does the final seven-year "week" begin on September 23, 2017? Thoughts?

That theory would stand to reason. We have been given several heavenly wonders, but this is the heavenly wonder that our LORD Jesus told us to watch for in Matthew 24, and the one that would cause the enemy to panic when they see the "woman in labor" discussed eighteen times in Scripture. It would coincide with Biblical prophecy, especially in Daniel 9, for the Battle of Armageddon to last seven years. Future will prove past.

Here's another interesting connection.
Daniel 9:27 says *"and in the **midst of the week** he shall cause the sacrifice and the oblation to cease."*
The **MIDST** of the week would be the **MIDDLE** - or 3 ½ years.

Get this interesting coincidence. Starting from the day President Trump was elected 11/8/2016, and counting forward 3 ½ years, is May 2020. That was when the hospital ships were in NY Harbor. Many believe the tunnels were cleared at that time. Many believe this was when the tunnels were cleared of child sacrifice and oblation to satan! Remember, President Trump said many times, "There's light at the end of the tunnel."

As always, future will prove past.
Patriots are READY!
WE WILL FIGHT UNTIL THE DAY OF VICTORY AND WE WILL TRUST THE PLAN!

9-REVELATION'S SEVEN STARS

"End Times and 1000 Years of Peace" Chapter 7
Revelation 1-7

1. What was our LORD telling us about our role and position in the earth? (Revelation 1:6)

> Revelation 1
> 6 *"He has made us a Kingdom of priests for God his Father. All glory and power to him forever and ever! Amen."*

Our destiny is to rule the earth and fill the earth with righteousness and praise to the LORD.

2. Decode Revelation 1:7

> Revelation 1
> 7 *"Look! He comes with the clouds of heaven. And everyone will see him— even those who pierced him. And all the nations of the world will mourn for him. Yes! Amen!"*

What do "clouds" represent? What does it mean that every eye shall see Him? Who are those who pierce him? Why would the nations of the earth mourn for him?

Clouds represent power and authority, so Christ will return to rule! Every eye will see Him means everyone will know Him and recognize Him as the King of the world.

I think it pierces our LORD if His own people fight against Him in the Great Battle of Armageddon. And they will mourn after the battle is over when they realize they were brainwashed to fight on the wrong side! Similar to the mourning in Zechariah 12:10-14 and the response to Elijah's showdown in 1 Kings 18:39.

3. What do the seven stars and seven lampstands (candlesticks) symbolize?

Revelation 1

12 "When I turned to see who was speaking to me, I saw seven gold lampstands.

13 And standing in the middle of the lampstands was someone like the Son of Man. He was wearing a long robe with a gold sash across his chest."

The stars and lampstands symbolize believers who are intended to light the world with God's glory.

4. How might our LORD have a voice as the sound of many waters, have eyes as a flame of fire, and a sharp two-edge sword out of his mouth?

Revelation 1

*14 "His head and his hair were white like wool, as white as snow. And **his eyes were like flames of fire.***

*15 His feet were like polished bronze refined in a furnace, and **his voice thundered like mighty ocean waves.***

*16 He held seven stars in his right hand, and a **sharp two-edged sword came from his mouth.** And his face was like the sun in all its brilliance."*

Many waters means our LORD speaks powerfully and everyone listens, even those who hate Him.

His eyes as flames of fire means He is taking vengeance on our enemies, and they fear Him!

The sharp two-edged sword out of His mouth indicates that the truth He tells about the NWO

criminal satanic cabal destroys them!

5. How does He hold the seven stars in his right hand? Write your thoughts about some other ways the LORD is described in Revelation 1.

I love that our LORD is standing in the midst of His people and holds us, His stars, in His right

hand of power. His face is bright with truth and hope! Even His head and hair are bright! He

emanates truth!

PLEIADES CORRELATION TO THE SEVEN CHURCHES IN ASIA MINOR ADDRESSED IN REVELATION CH. 2 & CH. 3

Note That The Star Of The Church Of Philadelphia, Which Is Given The Divine Promise That They Would ESCAPE The HOUR Of TRIAL In Rev. 3:10, Is Missing!

6. What is the significance of the formation in Asia-Minor of the seven churches John describes? (we will talk about this more in a later chapter of this study guide.)

Revelation 1

20 "This is the meaning of the mystery of the seven stars you saw in my right hand and the seven gold lampstands: The seven stars are the angels of the seven churches, and the seven lampstands are the seven churches."

Explain the significance of the locations of the seven original churches listed in Revelation 1.

The locations of the original seven churches in Asia Minor were in the exact formation of Pleiades, known as the seven sisters. The churches represent the stars in heaven that are in the heart of Taurus the Bull, which symbolizes our LORD Jesus coming on a rampage to rescue us.

7. Write some clues John gave us in Revelation 2 about the satan worshipers.

Revelation 2

10 "Don't be afraid of what you are about to suffer. The devil will throw some of you into prison to test you. You will suffer for ten days. But if you remain faithful even when facing death, I will give you the crown of life.

11 "Anyone with ears to hear must listen to the Spirit and understand what he is saying to the churches. Whoever is victorious will not be harmed by the second death.

12 "Write this letter to the angel of the church in Pergamum. This is the message from the one with the sharp two-edged sword:

13 "I know that you live in the city where satan has his throne, yet you have remained loyal to me. You refused to deny me even when Antipas, my faithful witness, was martyred among you there in satan's city.

*14 "But I have a few complaints against you. You tolerate some among you whose teaching is like that of Balaam, who showed Balak how to trip up the people of Israel. **He taught them to sin by eating food offered to idols and by committing sexual sin.***

15 In a similar way, you have some Nicolaitans among you who follow the same teaching."

John told us these demon-filled people will throw believers in prison and try to kill them. He told us they have authority in certain cities. He warned us that they are cannibals and sexual deviants.

8. What are some clues about the satan worshipers that John gave us in Revelation 3?

Revelation 3

*9 "Look, **I will force those who belong to Satan's synagogue—those liars who say they are Jews but are not—to come and bow down at your feet.** They will acknowledge that you are the ones I love."*

10 "Because you have obeyed my command to persevere, I will protect you from the great time of testing that will come upon the whole world to test those who belong to this world.

11 I am coming soon. Hold on to what you have, so that no one will take away your crown.

12 All who are victorious will become pillars in the Temple of my God, and they will never have to leave it. And I will write on them the name of my God, and they will be citizens in the city of my God—the new Jerusalem that comes down from heaven from my God. And I will also write on them my new name.

13 "Anyone with ears to hear must listen to the Spirit and understand what he is saying to the churches.

He told us they say they are Jews, but they are not. They are actually the synogogue of satan. He also told us that his warriors in Armageddon will be victorious and will be the foundation of New Jerusalem! The will even bear His New Name!

9. Tell how Revelation 2:25-29 makes you feel.

Revelation 2

25 "...hold tightly to what you have until I come.

26 To all who are victorious, who obey me to the very end, To them I will give authority over all the nations.

27 They will rule the nations with an iron rod
and smash them like clay pots.

28 They will have the same authority I received from my Father, and I will also give them the morning star!

29 "Anyone with ears to hear must listen to the Spirit and understand what he is saying to the churches."

This verse makes me excited about our future! To see our LORD destroy the wicked! To have the righteous rule on earth! We just have to hold on tight just a little longer!

10. In what condition is the church in Sardis? What does the LORD command them to do? What happens if they don't?

> Revelation 3
> 1 *"Write this letter to the angel of the church in Sardis. This is the message from the one who has the sevenfold Spirit of God and the seven stars:*
> *"I know all the things you do, and that you have a reputation for being alive—**but you are dead.***
> *2 Wake up! Strengthen what little remains, for even what is left is almost dead. I find that your actions do not meet the requirements of my God.*
> *3 Go back to what you heard and believed at first; hold to it firmly. Repent and turn to me again. **If you don't wake up, I will come to you suddenly, as unexpected as a thief."***

The church in Sardis is DEAD! They are not watching and listening carefully. They need to WAKE UP!! If they don't wake up, our LORD Jesus will come upon them suddenly and unexpectedly.

11. According to Revelation 3:3, what will happen if they DO watch? What will watching believers know and experience?

Those who are awake will recognize Christ's appearing! They will fight alongside Him! They will rejoice in the victory of Armageddon! They will know forever they were His chosen warriors!

12. Write down your thoughts about Revelation 3:9.

> Revelation 3
> 9 *"Look, **I will force those who belong to Satan's synagogue—those liars who say they are Jews but are not—to come and bow down at your feet.** They will acknowledge that you are the ones I love."*

The evildoers have literally taken the name Jew in vain. They have used that name for evil purposes, in order to rule over humanity. But they will be defeated and have to admit that we are the ones the LORD loves, and that He has rescued us from their evil clutches!

13. Thoughts on Revelation 3:12...specifically "I will write upon him MY NEW NAME."

Revelation 3

*12 "All who are victorious will become pillars in the Temple of my God, and they will never have to leave it. And I will write on them the name of my God, and they will be citizens in the city of my God—the new Jerusalem that comes down from heaven from my God. And I will also write on them **my new name**."*

Can you imagine having the LORD's name? This could literally be a legal name change, like being knighted! Imagine the blessing for your future progeny to be blessed with His NEW NAME! What Biblical name might that be?

14. How does Revelation 3:12 make you feel?

I'm so excited to be awake and fighting in the Battle of Armageddon! What an honor! What a blessing! That truth keeps me steady in the battle, trusting the plan! Humanity has been waiting for this Great Day and we are unspeakably blessed to see it and be a part of saving humanity!

15. Why was the LORD angry with the church of Laodicea? What does that say about professing faith? What does that indicate regarding the eternal security of believers – "once saved, always saved?" How can we tell if our faith is genuine?

Revelation 3

14 "Write this letter to the angel of the church in Laodicea. This is the message from the one who is the Amen—the faithful and true witness, the beginning of God's new creation:

15 "I know all the things you do, that you are neither hot nor cold. I wish that you were one or the other!"

16 "But since you are like lukewarm water, neither hot nor cold, I will spit you out of my mouth!

17 You say, 'I am rich. I have everything I want. I don't need a thing!' And you don't realize that you are wretched and miserable and poor and blind and naked.

18 So I advise you to buy gold from me—gold that has been purified by fire. Then you will be rich. Also buy white garments from me so you will not be shamed by your nakedness, and ointment for your eyes so you will be able to see.

19 I correct and discipline everyone I love. So be diligent and turn from your indifference.

20 "Look! I stand at the door and knock. If you hear my voice and open the door, I will come in, and we will share a meal together as friends.

21 Those who are victorious will sit with me on my throne, just as I was victorious and sat with my Father on his throne."

22 "Anyone with ears to hear must listen to the Spirit and understand what he is saying to the churches."

They were complacent. Indifferent to the suffering around them. They were too busy to be bothered to speak up for Christ or against the injustice. The LORD was not happy about that.

FOUR LIVING CREATURES DECODED!
Recorded in Revelation 4, John shows us a vision of heaven with the LORD sitting enthroned in brilliant splendor, with twenty-four elders clothed in white and wearing golden crowns, and four very strange creatures around the throne.

> Revelation 4
> *6 "In the center and around the throne were four living beings,*
> *each covered with eyes, front and back.*
> *7 The first of these living beings was like a lion; the second was like an ox;*
> *the third had a human face; and the fourth was like an eagle in flight.*
> *8 Each of these living beings had six wings, and their wings were covered all over with eyes,*
> *inside and out. Day after day and night after night they keep on saying,*
> *"Holy, holy, holy is the Lord God, the Almighty—*
> *the one who always was, who is, and who is still to come."*

This is very similar to the strange beings in Ezekiel 1:9-11.

> Ezekiel 1
> *9 "The wings of each living being touched the wings of the beings beside it.*
> *Each one moved straight forward in any direction without turning around.*
> *10 Each had a human face in the front, the face of a lion on the right side, the face of an ox*
> *on the left side, and the face of an eagle at the back.*
> *11 Each had two pairs of outstretched wings—one pair stretched out to touch the wings of*
> *the living beings on either side of it, and the other pair covered its body."*

16. List the four Living Beings in Revelation 4:7.

     Like a Lion   **Like an Ox**

   Had a Human Face   **Like an Eagle**

17. Where would we look to find the correct decode for the symbolism of these four Beings?

    The Bible!

18. Where would we not look? (human wisdom) **human wisdom and modern End Times teaching.**

19. Fill in the four Living Beings below. Then read Genesis 49 and see if any of these four

Beings are represented by Jacob's blessings on his children (tribes).

Living Being 1 *__Like a Lion__* represents the tribe of Israel ____*__Judah.__*

Living Being 2 *__Like an Ox__* represents the tribe of Israel __*__Ephraim.__*

Living Being 3 *__Had a Human Face__* represents the tribe of Israel *__Reuben.__*

Living Being 4 *__an Eagle__* represents the tribe of Israel____*__Dan.__*

Now check out this depiction of how the tribes of Israel always encamped in the wilderness.

20. Circle the major tribes for the north, south, east, and west.
Notice how each of the Four Living Beings matches the major tribes in the encampment!

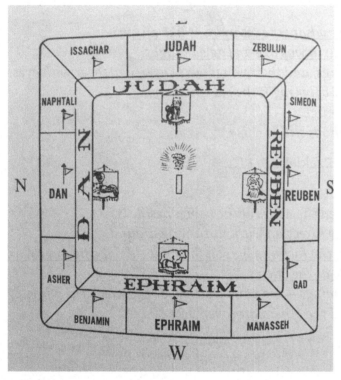

21. Who is in the middle of the camp?

__The LORD!__

That's it!
The strange 4 Living Beings represent God's people encircling the tabernacle of the LORD to worship Him!

Mystery Solved!

You will love this next decode too! In Revelation Chapter 5, John tells us of a vision in heaven where there is a sealed scroll that no one in heaven or earth or under the earth can open to reveal its contents. John knew the contents of that scroll held the key to setting the world free from the evil spiritual forces.

We will study the seven seals in the upcoming lessons. But for now, just know that the seals represent the mystery of how the world has been held in bondage to the evil one. John began to weep because he has lost hope that the world could ever be set free from satan's grip. If the seals can't be broken, the truth can't be revealed and satan can't be cast out...so humanity is hopeless. Come on, John! Where's your faith?!

> Revelation 5
> 5 *"But one of the twenty-four elders said to me, "Stop weeping! Look, the Lion of the tribe of Judah, the heir to David's throne, has won the victory. He is worthy to open the scroll and its seven seals.*
> *6 Then I saw a Lamb that looked as if it had been slaughtered, but it was now standing between the throne and the four living beings and among the twenty-four elders. He had seven horns and seven eyes, which represent the sevenfold Spirit of God that is sent out into every part of the earth."*

22. Who is the only one worthy to open the scroll and its seven seals? ___*Our LORD Jesus!*___
There IS hope.
Our LORD Jesus is worthy! He will save us!
Because our LORD Jesus was slaughtered and laid down His perfect, sinless life for us, He is worthy to stand between the throne of God and the four living beings. Those four living beings represent those who love God from every language and nation on earth. This verse is reminding us that our LORD Jesus stands as the mediator between God and men, reconciling us to God by His own precious blood.

The military operation we are all witnessing is the breaking of the seven seals that have held us in bondage. Our LORD Jesus is saving humanity right before our very eyes.

(For those who follow 17, take note that this verse is Revelation 5:5.
As in Clear Comms. Do you read this LOUD and CLEAR?)

23. Take a moment and praise Him with all the angels and believers surrounding the throne.

> Revelation 5
> 9 *"And they sang a new song with these words:*
> *"You are worthy to take the scroll and break its seals and open it.*
> *For you were slaughtered, and your blood has ransomed people for God from every tribe and language and people and nation.*
> *10 And you have caused them to become a Kingdom of priests for our God. And they will reign on the earth."*

11 Then I looked again, and I heard the voices of thousands and millions of angels around the throne and of the living beings and the elders.
12 And they sang in a mighty chorus:
"Worthy is the Lamb who was slaughtered—
to receive power and riches and wisdom and strength
and honor and glory and blessing."
13 And then I heard every creature in heaven and on
earth and under the earth and in the sea. They sang:
"Blessing and honor and glory and power
belong to the one sitting on the throne
and to the Lamb forever and ever.""

Lord I join with all creation praising You for rescuing us from the evil ones! You alone are worthy to receive the honor and praise forever! I praise You for laying down Your life and for coming to rescue pitiful brainwashed humanity. Thank You for waking us up and allowing us to join with You in this epic Battle of Armageddon. I can't wait for all the world to praise You!

In the next chapter in this Study Guide, the seals will be opened, revealing the truth about the satanic New World Order cabal. The LORD has helped us to see through the matrix of lies, and realize the evil forces that have been running the world. No doubt, the LORD Jesus has broken the seals and let us know the truth!

10-CONQUERING HORSES

"End Times and 1000 Years of Peace" Chapter 8
Revelation 6

In this chapter, Our LORD Jesus opens the seven seals that have held humanity in bondage. That's why we now know the satanic NWO cabal has run the world. Once the horses are decoded, it will make perfect sense to you! How did John describe each horse's rider?

1. White horse – ***This rider had a bow, and a crown, and went forth to conquer.***

2. Red horse - ***This rider had a mighty sword and the authority to take peace from the earth. And there was war and slaughter everywhere.***

3. Black horse - ***This rider was holding a pair of scales in his hand.***

4. Pale horse - ***This rider was named Death, and his companion was the Grave. These two were given authority over one-fourth of the earth, to kill with the sword and famine and disease and wild animals.***

Rather than representing an individual or a particular event, as you read Revelation 6, think of what the enemy does to destroy humanity.

Per Revelation 6:1-2, the rider on the white horse had a bow, and a crown, and went forth to conquer.

> Revelation 6
> *1 "As I watched, the Lamb broke the first of the seven seals on the scroll. Then I heard one of the four living beings say with a voice like thunder, "Come!"*
> *2 I looked up and saw a white horse standing there. Its rider carried a bow, and a crown was placed on his head. He rode out to win many battles and gain the victory."*

5. How did the rider on the white horse get a crown?

The crown was placed on his head, as if he did not earn it and was not worthy to rule.

6. What does a crown represent? *Authority, Rule*

7. Per Revelation 6:1-2, what does the rider on the white horse do?

He rode out to win many battles and gain the victory. As in conquer many people. NWO.

8. The white horse represents how the enemy tries to destroy humanity through:

Puppet leaders installed in governments and corporations and religious organizations all throughout the world.

9. Per Revelation 6:3-4, what was the rider on the red horse given?

> Revelation 6
> 3 "When the Lamb broke the second seal, I heard the second living being say, "Come!"
> 4 Then another horse appeared, a red one. Its rider was given a mighty sword and the authority to take peace from the earth. And there was war and slaughter everywhere."

A mighty sword and the authority to take peace from the earth.

10. The red horse represents how the enemy tries to destroy humanity through:

War and slaughter everywhere.

11. Per Revelation 6:5-6, what did the rider on black horse hold?

> Revelation 6
> 5 "When the Lamb broke the third seal, I heard the third living being say, "Come!" I looked up and saw a black horse, and its rider was holding a pair of scales in his hand.
> 6 And I heard a voice from among the four living beings say, "A loaf of wheat bread or three loaves of barley will cost a day's pay. And don't waste the olive oil and wine."

A pair of scales.

Usually a pair of scales, or balances, represents the justice system. But in this case, Revelation 6:6 gives us insight on their meaning.

12. What is proclaimed in Revelation 6:6? So what do the scales represent?

"A loaf of wheat bread or three loaves of barley will cost a day's pay. And don't waste the olive oil and wine." So these are marketplace scales, representing the financial system.

13. What is Revelation 6:6 telling us about the financial system run by the Beast?

The NWO controllers keep humanity in a financially stressed position, to cause them to suffer and to keep them from having time and resources to fight back. The people work all day for bread to eat, and can't afford to waste one thing!

14. What does oil (balm) represent in God's Word? *Healing and comfort.*

15. What does wine represent in God's Word? *Joy*

16. So what is the voice also saying to protect? *Protect your physical and mental health*

17. Thoughts? *We are all realizing how the NWO has damaged our physical health, and how they have even attacked our mental health in countless ways. Pure evil.*

18. The black horse represents how the enemy tries to destroy humanity through:

Lack and manipulation of the financial system, including currency manipulation.

19. What was the rider on the pale horse named? *Death.*

> Revelation 6
> 7 "When the Lamb broke the fourth seal, I heard the fourth living being say, "Come!"
> 8 I looked up and saw a horse whose color was pale green. Its rider was named Death, and his companion was the Grave. These two were given authority over one-fourth of the earth, to kill with the sword and famine and disease and wild animals."

20. What followed? Who was the companion of the pale horse?

The Grave .

21. What power was given to the rider on the pale horse?

Authority over one-fourth of the earth, to kill with the sword and famine and disease and wild animals.

What four ways does the rider on the pale horse take life? Give examples.

22. Sword - *Endless wars.*

23. Famine - *Deprivation and starvation worldwide, including under communism.*

24. Disease – *They actually created diseases and weakened our immune system to destroy us.*

25. Wild Animals – *I wonder if the wild animals are symbolically gangs like MS-13.*

26. Summarize how the pale horse represents how the enemy tries to destroy humanity.

The NWO has worked tirelessly to destroy humanity and take power through puppet leaders in every place of authority, endless wars, financial manipulation, and created diseases and pandemics. Now that we know who they are and what they have been doing to us, our only option is to destroy them!

27. Do you think these "horses" appear chronologically or simultaneously over years?
Simultaneously over years.

28. Who is driving these wild horses? *The NWO satanic criminal cabal.*

29. What are the ones in Revelation 6:9-10 crying to the LORD to do?

> Revelation 6
> 9 "When the Lamb broke the fifth seal, I saw under the altar the souls of all who had been martyred for the word of God and for being faithful in their testimony.
> 10 They shouted to the Lord and said, "O Sovereign Lord, holy and true, how long before you judge the people who belong to this world and avenge our blood for what they have done to us?"

Avenge our blood for what they have done to us!

30. Thoughts? Is this a righteous prayer? Why or why not?

Absolutely yes! We are calling on the LORD for righteousness on earth, for humanity to be rescued, and for the evildoers to be punished! Biblical!

31. What does Revelation 6:11 tell us about the suffering of God's people?

> Revelation 6
> 11 "Then a white robe was given to each of them. And they were told to rest a little longer until the full number of their brothers and sisters —their fellow servants of Jesus who were to be martyred—had joined them."

Even in heaven, they are asking the LORD to avenge their deaths! But the LORD tells them they have to wait until more are killed by the NWO. That sounds so strange, but it is necessary for humanity to awaken. And it means rewards for the righteous and judgment for the wicked.

Revelation 6:12-14 is the answer to their prayers for judgment to fall on the cabal!

> Revelation 6
> *12 "I watched as the Lamb broke the sixth seal, and there was a great earthquake. The sun became as dark as black cloth, and the moon became as red as blood.*
> *13 Then the stars of the sky fell to the earth like green figs falling from a tree shaken by a strong wind.*
> *14 The sky was rolled up like a scroll, and all of the mountains and islands were moved from their places."*

What are your thoughts on the following symbols in Revelation 6:12-14? Some might be physical, as in astronomical. Some might be symbolic.

32. Earthquake - *I believe that symbolizes the crumbling destruction of the NWO.*

33. Sun Black as Sackcloth - *The destruction of the NWO will be for them as if the sun went out! Hell is utter blackness and darkness. (2 Peter 2:4)*

34. Moon Became as Blood - *Blood moons which symbolize the NWO dark agenda being exposed and brought down.*

35. Stars of heaven fell to earth - *I believe the stars falling symbolize the NWO and their minions falling in the eyes of the people, as well as falling under judgment.*

36. Fig Tree casts her figs - *I believe this symbolizes those who have taken the name Jew in vain in order to oppress and destroy humanity. The fake fig tree is dying.*

37. Shaken in a Mighty Wind - *The LORD is the storm that is shaking the NWO AntiChrist!*

38. Heaven departed as a scroll rolled together - *This might symbolize chemtrails that are proof for everyone of their ongoing crimes against humanity. It might also symbolize that even they skies are calling for judgment to fall on them!*

39. Every Mountain and Island moved - *The high and low of the NWO will be destroyed.*

40. What do the kings and mighty men do in response to Revelation 6:12-14?

> Revelation 6

15 "Then everyone—the kings of the earth, the rulers, the generals, the wealthy, the powerful, and every slave and free person—all hid themselves in the caves and among the rocks of the mountains.

16 And they cried to the mountains and the rocks, "Fall on us and hide us from the face of the one who sits on the throne and from the wrath of the Lamb.

17 For the great day of their wrath has come, and who is able to survive?"

The powerful and the minions of the NWO hide and cry out to be hidden from God's judgment.

41. Who are they afraid of? ***They are afraid of the wrath of the Lamb, our Lord Jesus Christ.***

42. What do the kings prefer to happen to them rather than seeing the face of the Lamb?

They'd rather have the rocks and hills fall on them and crush them, annihilation, rather than look into the holy eyes of Jesus Christ under His judgment. They hate Him!

43. What does the "face of the Lamb" represent? ***Christ's anger toward the wicked for their unceasing unfathomable crimes against His bride. The NWO hates that He is their Judge.***

44. What do the kings recognize about Christ? ***They realize the Lord Jesus Christ has the power to judge and punish them, and that He will do it. Nothing can stop what is coming.***

So now that we have analyzed the wild horses of Revelation 6, it seems that the correct interpretation is that satan has been driving these wild horses since the beginning of time, to destroy humanity through evil dictators, war, lack, and disease. All the earth has suffered untold cruelty at their hands.

Thankfully, during the Millennial Kingdom on earth, the Beast, the False Prophet, and satan will be chained for 1,000 years! We will all have plenty of time to reflect on how dangerous it was for the world to allow satan to have any place on earth.

Take a moment and give praise to the LORD for not only saving us from eternal hell but also for saving the entire earth from satan's rule, and for coming to the world rule in righteousness!

I praise you LORD for being the wonderful King of the World! You alone can destroy the works of darkness and set us free! We are so excited to have You rule the world! Thank You for loving us and fighting for us and knowing the perfect plan!

11-KNIGHTHOOD

"End Times and 1000 Years of Peace" Chapter 9
Revelation 7

This chapter in Revelation was such a mystery to me! Why would the angels want to harm the earth? The answer is…They don't! Mystery solved! We will put this puzzle together one piece at a time. ENJOY!

1. At the opening of Revelation Chapter 7, four angels are standing at the:

Four corners of the earth, all over the entire world.

> Revelation 7
> 1 *"Then I saw four angels standing at the four corners of the earth, holding back the four winds so they did not blow on the earth or the sea, or even on any tree?"*

2. What are the angels holding? **_the four winds_** This symbolizes: **_the truth about the AntiChrist_**.

3. List some Scripture references where the phrase "four winds" is found.

Ezekiel 37:9, Daniel 7:2, Zechariah 6:5 says "The four spirits of heaven."

4. Based on these verses, what are the "four winds?"

The Holy Spirit who guides us into all truths from every side.

5. Based on 2 Thessalonians 2:6-8, what are the angels are holding back?

The truth about the AntiChrist- the man of lawlessness – also known as the NWO.

> 2 Thessalonians 2
> 6 *"And you know what is holding him back, for he can be revealed only when his time comes.*
> 7 *For this lawlessness is already at work secretly, and it will remain secret until the one who*

is holding it back steps out of the way.
8 Then the man of lawlessness will be revealed, but the Lord Jesus will slay him with the breath of his mouth and destroy him by the splendor of his coming."

6. Put together Revelation 7:1 and 2 Thessalonians 2:6-8, and explain what the angels are doing. (which seems like an odd job for an angel.)

The angels are holding back the truth.

7. Why are the angels holding back the "winds?"

Because humanity was not ready to know the truth yet. We had to wait until the Gospel had been proclaimed throughtout the entire world.

Once the winds are released and the man of lawlessness is revealed, it seems that our LORD Jesus destroys him quickly!

8. What are the four winds told to do in Ezekiel 37:9?

Ezekiel 37
9 "Then he said to me, "Speak a prophetic message to the winds, son of man. Speak a prophetic message and say, 'This is what the Sovereign Lord says: Come, O breath, from the four winds! Breathe into these dead bodies so they may live again.'"

Breathe into these dead bodies so they may live again. In other words, awaken humanity to fight the NWO!

9. How does the wind release compare in Revelation 7:1 and Ezekiel 37:9?

Both passages talk about the LORD giving the command to awaken humanity. The truth was held back for a long, long time, until the time was right. The truth was released so humanity can live again!

10. Are the winds or angels intended to harm humanity?

Revelation 7
2 "And I saw another angel coming up from the east, carrying the seal of the living God. And he shouted to those four angels, who had been given power to harm land and sea,"

The "harm" is because the truth hurts. The redpill about the NWO's crimes makes us sick. They are not telling us to harm us, but to deliver us.

11. Why would there be concern about the wind harming the earth? (think humanity being ready for the Great Awakening)

If the people woke up en masse too soon, the enemy would likely destroy them and prevent the

true worldwide Great Awakening from ever happening. Timing is everything.

12. The wind is not allowed to blow until what happens?

> Revelation 7
> *3 "Wait! Don't harm the land or the sea or the trees until we have placed the seal of God on the foreheads of his servants."*

Until the chosen warriors have the seal of God on their foreheads.

13. What does this indicate? *The chosen warriors are protected by the LORD for this battle, to*

accomplish His purpose.

14. Who were sealed?

> Revelation 7
> *4 "And I heard how many were marked with the seal of God—144,000 were sealed from all the tribes of Israel:*
> *5 Of the tribe of Judah were sealed twelve thousand. Of the tribe of Reuben were sealed twelve thousand. Of the tribe of Gad were sealed twelve thousand.*
> *6 Of the tribe of Asher were sealed twelve thousand. Of the tribe of Nephthali were sealed twelve thousand. Of the tribe of Manassah were sealed twelve thousand.*
> *7 Of the tribe of Simeon were sealed twelve thousand. Of the tribe of Levi were sealed twelve thousand. Of the tribe of Issachar were sealed twelve thousand.*
> *8 Of the tribe of Zebulon were sealed twelve thousand. Of the tribe of Joseph were sealed twelve thousand. Of the tribe of Benjamin were sealed twelve thousand."*

The LORD sealed the perfect number from the true tribes of Israel.

15. What is the significance of the tribes?

These are God's chosen warriors, who are Israelites by faith. Some are Abraham's physical

progeny from the scattered tribes. Some are not. All hear from God and follow Him.

16. What is the significance of the number 144,000?

12,000 from the 12 tribes of Israel. A perfect number.

17. Do you think 144,000 is an exact number or symbolic?

__Symbolic. I think the actual number is more like 200 million. "I heard the size of their army, which was 200 million mounted troops." (Revelation 9:16)__

18. These 144,000 might be the physical progeny of Abraham or might not be.
What is the defining characteristic of these 144,000 according to Galatians 3:7?

> Galatians 3
> 7 *"The real children of Abraham, then, are those who put their faith in God."*

__The defining characteristic of the 144,000 is faith. They listen to the LORD and follow Him wherever He leads them.__

19. Who is the great multitude described in Revelation 7:9?

> Revelation 7
> 9 *"After this I saw a vast crowd, too great to count, from every nation and tribe and people and language, standing in front of the throne and before the Lamb. They were clothed in white robes and held palm branches in their hands."*

__God's people from all time who love Him and worship Him, but they were not the chosen 144,000.__

20. The end of Revelation 7 is a praise hymn to the LORD who has promised to rescue humanity from the grip of the evil one.
These were victorious in the Great Tribulation! I believe he is talking not just about a seven-year period, but about the Great Tribulation that has happened since sin came into the world and satan began to rule as the prince of the power of the air.

Let's take this opportunity to praise the LORD.

> Revelation 7
> 10 *"And they were shouting with a great roar,*
> *"Salvation comes from our God who sits on the throne and from the Lamb!"*
> *11 And all the angels were standing around the throne and around the elders and the four living beings. And they fell before the throne with their faces to the ground and worshiped God.*
> *12 They sang, "Amen! Blessing and glory and wisdom*
> *and thanksgiving and honor*
> *and power and strength belong to our God*

forever and ever! Amen.”
13 Then one of the twenty-four elders asked me, “Who are these who are clothed in white?
Where did they come from?”
14 And I said to him, “Sir, you are the one who knows.”
Then he said to me, “These are the ones who died in the great tribulation.
They have washed their robes in the blood of the Lamb and made them white.
15 “That is why they stand in front of God’s throne
and serve him day and night in his Temple.
And he who sits on the throne will give them shelter.
16 They will never again be hungry or thirsty;
they will never be scorched by the heat of the sun.
17 For the Lamb on the throne will be their Shepherd.
He will lead them to springs of life-giving water.
And God will wipe every tear from their eyes.”

__Thank you LORD that our robes have been washed in Your blood. You have made us spotless!__

__We will stand in front of Your throne and serve You day and night in Your Temple.__

__You alone sit on the throne!__

__You have made a such a beautiful future for us and You will wipe every tear from our eyes.__

__Thank You, Lord!__

12-TRUMPET BLASTS

"End Times and 1000 Years of Peace" Chapter 10
Revelation 8 & 9

The Revelation 8 and 9 trumpet blasts were very confusing to me...likely because I had been so brainwashed into thinking the earth would be destroyed in the Battle of Armageddon. And as hard as you try, until most of the pieces come together about End Times prophecy, it's still so get hard to come out of brainwashing. In the first release of the book "End Times and 1000 Years of Peace," I got it wrong! So I inserted this corrected chapter in the revised book and on the *FreedomForce.LIVE* website.

Let the decoding begin!

Here's my favorite key to understanding these difficult passages in the Book of Revelation. Read the end first! (I actually didn't use this trick to discover the truth about the Trumpets, but I realize now that I should have!) Take a look at the Seventh Angel Trumpet blast! It's way over in Revelation Chapter 11. (Of course, the chapters were not inserted until long after John penned the Revelation.)

Here's the Seventh Angel Trumpet blast:

> Revelation 11
> *15 "Then the seventh angel blew his trumpet, and there were loud voices shouting in heaven: "The world has now become the Kingdom of our Lord and of his Christ, and he will reign forever and ever."*
> *16 The twenty-four elders sitting on their thrones before God fell with their faces to the ground and worshiped him.*
> *17 And they said, "We give thanks to you, Lord God, the Almighty, the one who is and who always was, for now you have assumed your great power and have begun to reign."*
> *18 "The nations were filled with wrath, but now the time of your wrath has come. It is time to judge the dead and reward your servants the prophets, as well as your holy people, and all who fear your name, from the least to the greatest. It is time to destroy all who have caused destruction on the earth."*

1. What is the seventh and final trumpet blast?

The LORD Jesus assumes His role as King of the World and begins to reign on earth!

2. Who is unhappy and why?

The nations (NWO) are filled with anger/wrath because the time of God's wrath has come. They

are unhappy because they are under judgment and the LORD is ruling the earth!

3. Who is happy and why?

Those who love God are happy because the LORD is ruling earth and He cast out the evildoers!

4. Here's a great clue on what the angels are doing with these trumpet blasts! It's the End Times for them and 1,000 years of peace for us!!! Trumpets are used all throughout God's Word! List some occasions in the Bible when trumpets were used.

To bring down the walls of Jericho; When Gideon's 300 destroyed the Midianites; Priests would

blow trumpets before the Ark of God; Trumpets were blown during the Feast of Trumpets to

gather the people together; Trumpets were blown to gather warriors to battle.

5. What was the purpose of the Feast of Trumpets? (see Leviticus 23)

To gather the people for the new year celebration, for repentance and for harvest.

6. Imagine you're sound asleep and someone blast the trumpet and your ears...

What's going to happen? *You will WAKE UP!*

And there you have it. **The Great Awakening.**

7. Notice Revelation 8:1 There was silence in heaven for half an hour before the trumpet blasts.

> Revelation 8
> 1 *"When the Lamb broke the seventh seal on the scroll, there was silence throughout heaven for about half an hour."*

Why? *I think all of Heaven stopped to pray silently for us. They know this is not a game. We are*

literally fighting demons.

8. Why were seven angels given incense in Revelation 8:3-5? What does the incense represent?

Revelation 8

2 "I saw the seven angels who stand before God, and they were given seven trumpets.

3 Then another angel with a gold incense burner came and stood at the altar. And a great amount of incense was given to him to mix with the prayers of God's people as an offering on the gold altar before the throne.

4 The smoke of the incense, mixed with the prayers of God's holy people, ascended up to God from the altar where the angel had poured them out.

5 Then the angel filled the incense burner with fire from the altar and threw it down upon the earth; and thunder crashed, lightning flashed, and there was a terrible earthquake."

The incense represents the Spirit of the LORD sanctifying our prayers as in Romans 8:26, "And the Holy Spirit helps us in our weakness. For example, we don't know what God wants us to pray for. But the Holy Spirit prays for us with groanings that cannot be expressed in words." The angels are given the incense to answer our prayers to destroy the NWO AntiChrist.

9. Before we attempt to decode what each of the trumpet blasts represents, what is the purpose for the trumpet blasts? Think Awakening. Think Battle.

Revelation 8

6 "Then the seven angels with the seven trumpets prepared to blow their mighty blasts."

The trumpet blasts are awakening humanity and calling them to battle!

The trumpets are awakening humanity not only to the horrifying abject evil... but to specifically **WHO** is responsible for the crimes against humanity?

10. In verse 7 we get the first clue as to WHO has been inflicting all the suffering on humanity.

Revelation 8

*7 "The first angel blew his trumpet, and hail and fire mixed with blood were thrown down on the earth. **One-third** of the earth was set on fire, **one-third** of the trees were burned, and all the green grass was burned."*

THE 33'S DID IT!

What is that clue? **_One-third of this, One-third of that, One-third of the other._**

11. 1/3 = _**33**_ %

12. 33% points us to 33 _**Degrees**_

13. 33° points us to **_Secret Societies working covertly against humanity._**

And now you know who has been causing all the havoc on earth. (NOTE: since there are varying levels of understanding in these secret societies, each person is not responsible for the overall evil that has been perpetrated.)

14. To answer the following questions, what might each of these angel trumpet blasts represent?

(I've put my thoughts in the book, "End Times and 1000 Years of Peace," but there are likely a wide range of possibilities for each, because their destruction has been so immense.)

15. First Angel Trumpet - ___All living things great and small worldwide are under attack by the NWO AntiChrist.___

16. Second Angel Trumpet – ___The NWO mountain/pyramid's crimes are finally being exposed before the world, so they will be destroyed. They have taken over the world's sea of commerce so the rest of humanity suffers lack.___

> Revelation 8
> 8 "Then the second angel blew his trumpet, and a great mountain of fire was thrown into the sea. **One-third** of the water in the sea became blood.
> 9 **One-third** of all things living in the sea died, and **one-third** of all the ships on the sea were destroyed."
> **THE 33'S DID IT!**

17. Third Angel Trumpet – ___The NWO poisoned the waters, causing humanity to become chronically ill and to not be able to think clearly.___

> Revelation 8
> 10 "Then the third angel blew his trumpet, and a great star fell from the sky, burning like a torch. It fell on **one-third** of the rivers and on the springs of water.
> 11 The name of the star was Bitterness. It made **one-third** of the water bitter, and many people died from drinking the bitter water."
> **THE 33'S DID IT!**

18. Fourth Angel Trumpet – ___This likely symbolizes the chemtrails covering up the sun, moon, and stars, poisoning our air. And they also covered up the heavenly wonders so we could not understand the signs the LORD put there for us.___

> Revelation 8
> 12 "Then the fourth angel blew his trumpet, and one-third of the sun was struck, and one-

third of the moon, and one-third of the stars, and they became dark. And one-third of the day was dark, and also one-third of the night."

THE 33'S DID IT!

NOTE: The Fifth Trumpet is also called the First Terror or First Woe.

> Revelation 8
> *13 "Then I looked, and I heard a single eagle crying loudly as it flew through the air, "Terror, terror, terror to all who belong to this world because of what will happen when the last three angels blow their trumpets."*

19. Fifth Angel Trumpet – ***The demonic locusts were released from the pits of hell to deceive humanity with countless lies from the media, intended to enslave us completely under NWO tyranny.***

> Revelation 9
> *1 "Then the fifth angel blew his trumpet, and I saw a star that had fallen to earth from the sky, and he was given the key to the shaft of the bottomless pit.*
> *2 When he opened it, smoke poured out as though from a huge furnace, and the sunlight and air turned dark from the smoke.*
> *3 Then locusts came from the smoke and descended on the earth, and they were given power to sting like scorpions."*

THE 33'S DID IT!

20. After the Fifth Angel Trumpet, there was a command given to the locusts.

> Revelation 9
> *4 "They were told not to harm the grass or plants or trees, but only the people who did not have the seal of God on their foreheads."*

During the battle of Armageddon, what is one of the greatest blessings of having the seal of God on our foreheads?

We see through the media's lies! So we are not harmed by their demonic propaganda! Thank You LORD!!!

21. Revelation 9:5-11 has one of the strangest depiction of our enemy ever! I put my thoughts in the book that these locusts are Fake News! What do you think?

> Revelation 9
> *5 "They were told not to kill them but to torture them for five months with pain like the pain of a scorpion sting.*
> *6 In those days people will seek death but will not find it. They will long to die, but death will flee from them!*

7 The locusts looked like horses prepared for battle. They had what looked like gold crowns on their heads, and their faces looked like human faces.
8 They had hair like women's hair and teeth like the teeth of a lion.
9 They wore armor made of iron, and their wings roared like an army of chariots rushing into battle.
10 They had tails that stung like scorpions, and for five months they had the power to torment people.
11 Their king is the angel from the bottomless pit; his name in Hebrew is Abaddon, and in Greek, Apollyon—the Destroyer."

22. What could Revelation 9:5-6 mean?

The MSM propaganda is literally a torture-chamber of lies. They are constantly stinging us with deception, and it's almost impossible to escape it. The five months is likely symbolic for a short period of time. Amazingly, despite their best efforts to cause humanity to end it all, we haven't. Of course, some have. But somehow the LORD is giving us collective hope that change is around the corner. Death is fleeing from us! Praise the LORD!

23. Thoughts on these locusts being prepared for battle?

Every day the mainstream media gets their talking points to deceive the public. Listening to them is literally going into a mental battlefield. Most don't make it out without being tricked! And they don't even know it!

24. Locusts whose heads were as crowns like gold and faces like the faces of men?

The MSM locusts consider themselves aabove us. They look human, but they aren't. They're demons.

25. Thoughts on hair like women and teeth of lions?

The MSM looks so outwardly beautiful, but their aim is to trick us into the NWO tyranny trap. They really are the enemy of the people.

26. Tails like scorpions and stings in their tails and power to hurt men five months? (remember, many times in Revelation, periods of time are not exact, but are meant to give a proportion of time)

MSM, like scorpions, are experts at surprise attacks. You're have a normal day, and pow! You get stung by their deception, and you never even saw it coming!

27. No matter what the symbols represent, we know that their king is who?

apollyon – abaddon – satan. This is literally a spiritual battle and that's why we need the seal of God's protection so desperately!

28. The Fifth Angel Trumpet is also called the first **TERROR or WOE**

29. The Sixth Angel Trumpet is also called the **SECOND TERROR or WOE**

30. Revelation 9:12-13, the Sixth Angel sounded the trumpet and the voice came from where?

> Revelation 9
> *12 "The first terror is past, but look, two more terrors are coming!*
> *13 Then the sixth angel blew his trumpet, and I heard a voice speaking from the four horns of the gold altar that stands in the presence of God."*

From the four horns of the gold altar.

31. What is the significance here of the four horns of the gold altar?

This is the place of mercy. If your life was in danger, you could place your hand on the horns of the altar, like a heavenly home base, and be safe.

32. What does the voice from the altar tell the Sixth Angel Trumpet to do?

14 "And the voice said to the sixth angel who held the trumpet, "Release the four angels who are bound at the great Euphrates River."

Release the four angels who are bound at the great Euphrates River.

33. These angels have been prepared for an hour and a day and a month and a year to slay the third part of men. This is a very specific date with a very specific purpose.

> Revelation 9
> *15 "Then the four angels who had been prepared for this hour and day and month and year were turned loose to kill **one-third** of all the people on earth.*

16 I heard the size of their army, which was 200 million mounted troops."

What is their purpose?

To slay the third part of men.

Nothing Can Stop What Is Coming! Praise the Lord!!

34. Who is being destroyed by the Sixth Angel Trumpet blast? (33) (Hint: See Revelation 9:20-21)

1/3's – the 33's - AKA 33 degrees – as in the 1/3 angels/demons who fell from heaven. The holy angels are slaying the NWO secret societies who have worked covertly to destroy humanity.

35. The angels are awakening God's Army to fight this battle!! What is the number of the army in Revelation 9:16? Thoughts?

200 Million mounted troops. This is likely close to the actual number of God's awakened army. It sounds like a huge number, and it is. But it is a fraction of humanity.

36. This is John's vision of God's Army being released to destroy the wicked!
    Revelation 9
    17 "And in my vision, I saw the horses and the riders sitting on them. The riders wore armor that was fiery red and dark blue and yellow. The horses had heads like lions, and fire and smoke and burning sulfur billowed from their mouths.
    18 One-third of all the people on earth were killed by these three plagues—by the fire and smoke and burning sulfur that came from the mouths of the horses.
    19 Their power was in their mouths and in their tails. For their tails had heads like snakes, with the power to injure people."

37. What is the significance of God's Army's power being in their mouth?

Our mouths speak powerful truth to expose the enemy! We are breathing out fiery truth on social media daily!

38. What is the significance of God's Army's power being in their tails?

We are striking them when they least expect it! It happens time after time. The NWO attacks us, but we turn it around expose it on social media! Boomerang! They never learn!

39. What does God's Army's fire represent?

__Fiery judgment from God's altar.__

40. What does smoke represent?

__The Holy Spirit Who empowers us.__

41. What does brimstone represent?

__Our red-hot condemnation of the NWO's crimes.__

> Revelation 9
> *20 "But the people who did not die in these plagues still refused to repent of their evil deeds and turn to God. They continued to worship demons and idols made of gold, silver, bronze, stone, and wood—idols that can neither see nor hear nor walk!*
> *21 And they did not repent of their murders or their witchcraft or their sexual immorality or their thefts."*

42. Do the evildoers repent?

__No. They are held captive by satan.__

We are fighting pure evil demonic forces. They have literally blasphemed the Holy Spirit, which means they cast out the Holy Spirit and took in demonic spirits to be controlled by them. It is also called the unpardonable sin, and the sin unto death. This sin is unforgivable because the person is controlled by the demonic forces, and therefore refuses to repent.

43. What does it mean to blaspheme the Holy Spirit?

__To cast out the Holy Spirit and take in demonic spirits to be controlled by them.__

44. What are two other names in Scripture for blasphemy of the Holy Spirit?

__"The Blasphemy of the Holy Spirit" and "The Sin unto Death" (1 John 5:16-17)__

45. Are all sins the same in God's eyes?

__No. That was major deception.__

46. The Lord promised us in 2 Thessalonians is 2:8-12 what would happen to those who worship satan. Write your thoughts on their just punishment.

> 2 Thessalonians 2
> *8 "Then the man of lawlessness will be revealed, but the Lord Jesus will slay him with the breath of his mouth and destroy him by the splendor of his coming.*

9 This man will come to do the work of satan with counterfeit power and signs and miracles.

10 He will use every kind of evil deception to fool those on their way to destruction, because they refuse to love and accept the truth that would save them.

11 So God will cause them to be greatly deceived, and they will believe these lies.

12 Then they will be condemned for enjoying evil rather than believing the truth."

The Lord Jesus will slay him (NWO AntiChrist) with the breath of his mouth and destroy him by the splendor of his coming. That is why nothing can stop what is coming. They were greatly deceived into joining with the dark forces. And they loved evil rather than loving the LORD. They have been fully consumed with evil and must be removed from the earth.

Praise the LORD for ridding the world of those who are filled with demons!

13-REDPILLED

"End Times and 1000 Years of Peace" Chapter 11
Revelation 10

As usual, before the Great Awakening, Revelation 10 was impossible for me to understand. But now that we have experienced the Great Awakening, it makes so much more sense. Let's briefly go over clues to decode Revelation Chapter 10.

We see the seventh angel, but he doesn't sound his trumpet until Revelation Chapter 11.

1. Write the possible significance of the symbolism in Revelation 10:1.

> Revelation 10
> 1 *"Then I saw another mighty angel coming down from heaven, surrounded by a cloud, with a rainbow over his head. His face shone like the sun, and his feet were like pillars of fire."*

A mighty angel clothed with a cloud –

This angel message is about the power and authority of Almighty God to save humanity from the demons.

Rainbow over his head -

Revealing the promise of God not to destroy the earth.

Face shone like the sun -

Full of truth (Mercury is closest to the sun)

Feet as pillars of fire -

Fast moving angel (Mercury is the fastest moving "wandering star.")

2. Why does this angel have an open book?

Revelation 10
2 "And in his hand was a small scroll that had been opened. He stood with his right foot on the sea and his left foot on the land."

Because Jesus broke the seal and opened the scroll to start the Great Awakening and the Battle of Armageddon!

3. Later we will discuss the Beast of the sea (New World Order Beast) and the Beast of the land (False Prophets). Why might this angel have his feet on the sea and on the land?

Because his message is to both tyrants of the sea and the land, and to all their victims.

4. Any ideas on why the angel did not sound a trumpet (yet) but cried out with a loud voice like a lion?

Revelation 10
3 "And he gave a great shout like the roar of a lion. And when he shouted, the seven thunders answered.
4 When the seven thunders spoke, I was about to write. But I heard a voice from heaven saying, "Keep secret what the seven thunders said, and do not write it down."

This is what humanity has been waiting for… the eradication of the the beast, the false prophet, and satan from the earth. The Lion roars like the Universal Studios lion, as if to say, "Get ready for the movie of all time!"

5. Why does the angel say "there will be no more delay," and when the angel begins to blow the trumpet, God's mysterious plan will be fulfilled? (Revelation 10:6-7)

Revelation 10
6 "He swore an oath in the name of the one who lives forever and ever, who created the heavens and everything in them, the earth and everything in it, and the sea and everything in it.
He said, "There will be no more delay.
7 When the seventh angel blows his trumpet, God's mysterious plan will be fulfilled. It will happen just as he announced it to his servants the prophets."

He's saying "Get Ready Everybody!" Once he blows the seventh trumpet, that's it! God's mysterious plan will be fulfilled, satan will be cast out, and the earth will be ruled by our LORD

__Jesus Christ!__

6. What was John told to do in Revelation 10:8?

> Revelation 10
> *8 "Then the voice from heaven spoke to me again: "Go and take the open scroll from the hand of the angel who is standing on the sea and on the land."*

__Go get the scroll that Jesus opened.__

7. What did the angel tell John in verse 9?

> Revelation 10
> *9 "So I went to the angel and told him to give me the small scroll. "Yes, take it and eat it," he said. "It will be sweet as honey in your mouth, but it will turn sour in your stomach!"*
> *10 So I took the small scroll from the hand of the angel, and I ate it! It was sweet in my mouth, but when I swallowed it, it turned sour in my stomach."*

__The angel told John to eat the scroll.__

8. Did the angel warn John? How?

__The angel told John the scroll would taste sweet but it would make him nauseas.__

9. How might the book be sweet as honey in John's mouth?

__So many questions he's had will be answered. Everything will start to make sense!__

10. How might the book make John's belly bitter?

__The truth about what NWO AntiChrist's crimes against humanity will make him sick.__

11. Have you experienced something like this? Explain.

__Yes. I have had a voracious appetite to discover the truth. But every time I discover the truth about a topic, it makes me sick to know what they have done to humanity!__

12. What assignment was given to John?

> Revelation 10
> *10 "Then I was told, "You must prophesy again about many peoples, nations, languages, and kings."*

__John was to speak the truth to a wide array of people.__

13. Do we have a similar assignment? Explain.

__Yes. We who are awake have the responsibility to share the truth we have learn as far and wide__

__as we possibly can.__

14. What is the word we use to describe what happened to John? (Hint – Melly's channel name and also the title of this chapter.) If you're unfamiliar with that word, see the "Matrix" movie.)

__Redpilled!__

14-THE TWO WITNESSES

"End Times and 1000 Years of Peace" Chapter 12
Revelation 11

Revelation Chapter 11 has more symbolism then almost any other part of Revelation. The Lord had a good reason why He didn't tell us straight out who the Two Witnesses are. But He did give us lots of clues!

Think of it like a big jigsaw puzzle that is really hard to put together. That's what I did, using every bit of Bible knowledge I could scrape together. I would recommend that you read the *The Two Witnesses* chapter in the book *"End Times and 1000 Years of Peace"* before you attempt this study. For the sake of saving you time and frustration, I will go ahead and tell you that I am convinced that the Two Witnesses are not individuals, but are <u>"the church and the state," also known as the religious institutions and the government institutions.</u> That will make this study guide chapter much easier. It's like having the picture for a jigsaw puzzle…but you still have to put the pieces together!

I'm going to ask some questions.
Answer them the best you can. Don't worry if you can't answer them all.
At the end I will give a summary of this chapter so you can fill in some blanks that you might not know the answer to. But I don't want to spoil all your fun in working the puzzle!!

> Revelation 11
> *1 "Then I was given a measuring stick, and I was told, "Go and measure the Temple of God and the altar, and count the number of worshipers.*
> *2 But do not measure the outer courtyard, for it has been turned over to the nations. They will trample the holy city for 42 months."*

1. What was John told to measure?

The Temple of God, the altar, and to count the worshipers.

2. What is the purpose of measuring? (it was not about dimensions)
To determine the worshipers' devotion to the LORD.

3. What was John supposed to leave out?

Those who were near the temple, but not worshipers.

4. Why?

It's time for the Great Awakening and he needs to know if the worshipers are ready.

5. What does it mean that the holy city would be tread under foot?

Those who believe in God but are not yet awakened, (by keeping their lamps trimmed), will be tricked by the NWO AntiChrist's lies.

6. What does the 42 months' days usually signify?

A period of battle.

> Revelation 11
> 3 "And I will give power to my two witnesses, and they will be clothed in burlap and will prophesy during those 1,260 days.
> 4 These two prophets are the two olive trees and the two lampstands that stand before the Lord of all the earth.

7. What are the Two Witnesses wearing?

Burlap, mourning clothes.

Why? *They are distraught over the oppression and the wars and the evil on earth.*

8. Revelation 11:4 tells us these Witnesses are the two olive trees and the two candlesticks… clearly symbolic. What are olive trees and candlesticks used for?

Olives – *Healing and Comfort.*

For hints, see Psalm 52:8 -"I am like an olive tree flourishing in the house of God." And see Psalm 104:15 "wine to make them glad, olive oil to soothe their skin, and bread to give them strength."

9. Candlesticks – *Lighting the way.*

10. Specifically, what roles are these witnesses to perform on earth?

They are supposed to make sure everyone is treated fairly with justice, and that the truth is clear to everyone.

11. Do you think the 1,260 days' time frame is literal or symbolic? *Symbolic*

12. Clue about the first Witness. Who in the Bible was given power to shut up the heaven so

it would not rain? (clue from James 5:17-18) *Elijah*

13. What group or institution does the 1st Witness represent?

Elijah represents the Prophets. So the First Witness represents the Religious Institutions (or the

Church).

14. Clue about the second Witness. Who in the Bible was given power to turn water into blood and smite the earth with plagues? (For a hint, see Exodus 4:9 and Deuteronomy 28:59)

Moses.

15. What group or institution does the second Witness represent?

Moses represents the law or the Government Instutions (the State).

16. So who do the Two Witnesses represent?

The *Church* and the *State.*

17. What power do these institutions have? In what ways can they exercise those powers?

> Revelation 11
> 5 *"If anyone tries to harm them, fire flashes from their mouths and consumes their enemies. This is how anyone who tries to harm them must die.*
> 6 *They have power to shut the sky so that no rain will fall for as long as they prophesy. And they have the power to turn the rivers and oceans into blood, and to strike the earth with every kind of plague as often as they wish."*

They have the power to consume and execute their enemies.

18. Recently, have these Two Witnesses/institutions fulfilled their roles to protect God's people and to bring judgment on evildoers?

No. They have failed miserably due to infiltration.

Revelation 11:7-10 has very odd symbolism. Read the passage and then try to answer the following questions.

> Revelation 11
> 7 *"When they complete their testimony, the beast that comes up out of the bottomless pit will declare war against them, and he will conquer them and kill them.*
> 8 *And their bodies will lie in the main street of Jerusalem, the city that is figuratively called "Sodom" and "Egypt," the city where their Lord was crucified.*
> 9 *And for three and a half days, all peoples, tribes, languages, and nations will stare at their bodies. No one will be allowed to bury them.*
> 10 *All the people who belong to this world will gloat over them and give presents to each other to celebrate the death of the two prophets who had tormented them."*

19. What does it mean that the Two Witnesses "finished their testimony?" Is that good or bad?

To finish their testimony means to stop testifying to the truth and lies take over. This is very _bad._

20. The Beast came up from the pit to make war against these Two Witnesses only after they had finished their testimony. The Beast "killed" them. Revelation 11:8 says their bodies lie dead in Sodom and Egypt. What two significant sins were these locations known for? Of course, our Lord Jesus' precious blood even pays for these sins, for those who repent.

Sodom – _Sexual deviancy_

Egypt – _Tyranny_

21. What two significant sins is the New World Order known for?

Sexual deviancy and _Tyranny._
(In other words, Revelation 11:8 says these heinous sins have been used to enable the Beast to take over the Church and State.)

22. Specifically why were the Two Witnesses' bodies not buried?

Because the NWO wanted it to appear that the Church and the State are operating normally.

They might only need a few tweaks here and there. If the NWO shut down the Church and State,

that would wake up the sleeping giant!

23. The "earth-dwellers" (verse 10) celebrated. Who are they? (compared to heaven-dwellers)

Earth-dwellers in this section refers to those who are filled with demons. They do not think godly

thoughts, but demonic thoughts.

24. Why? _They celebrated because with the Church and State under NWO control, they could get_

away with their crimes Scot Free!

25. How long are the Two Witnesses' bodies "dead" symbolically?

3 ½ days

(Hints - Symbolism - 42 months = 1260 days = 3 ½ years (3 ½ days) = Time, Times, and Half a Time = Period of Striving/Battle = Jupiter / Melchizedek loop.)

26. How had the Two Witnesses/prophets tormented those who dwelt on the earth (demon-worshipers)?

By holding them accountable for their sins/crimes.

27. Write in your own words what miracle happened in verse 11.

God woke up His Two Witnesses! He woke us up to tell us the truth about the NWO and for us to spread the truth, which is our role!

> Revelation 11
> *11 "But after three and a half days, God breathed life into them, and they stood up! Terror struck all who were staring at them.*
> *12 Then a loud voice from heaven called to the two prophets, "Come up here!" And they rose to heaven in a cloud as their enemies watched.*
> *13 At the same time there was a terrible earthquake that destroyed a tenth of the city. Seven thousand people died in that earthquake, and everyone else was terrified and gave glory to the God of heaven."*

28. We call this event: ***The Great Awakening!***

29. What effect does this have on those who saw them? (Revelation 11:11)

The NWO was struck with terror! The sleeping giant has awakened! And they won't stop until NWO is destroyed!

30. Which Old Testament passages does Revelation 11:11 remind you of?

 Ezekiel 37 and *Joel 2* .

(Hint - take a minute and reread Ezekiel 37 and Joel 2, and compare to Revelation 11:11)

Thoughts on comparison?

Ezekiel 37 tells of the wind breathing on the slain, and they rise up a mighty army, just like us!

Joel 2 tells about a mighty army appearing seemingly out of nowhere, lead by Christ Himself!

31. What could "rose to heaven in a cloud" mean symbolically? (Revelation 11:12)
Ascend to positions of power and authority.

32. What are God's people raised up to high positions to do? (see Revelation 11:12 & 20:6)
Whether in government or education or social media platforms or religious institutions or entertainment or any other role you can think of. We will reign with Christ!

33. Revelation 11:13 rocks the world! What happens?

A terrifying earthquake of judgment destroys the NWO cabal. Everyone sees it and repents.

34. All of heaven breaks out into the Hallelujah Chorus! Describe what it will be like when Christ takes His seat of authority as the King of the World and reigns on earth! Revelation 11:15-17

> Revelation 11
> 14 *"The second terror is past, but look, the third terror is coming quickly.*
> 15 *Then the seventh angel blew his trumpet, and there were loud voices shouting in heaven: "The world has now become the Kingdom of our Lord and of his Christ, and he will reign forever and ever."*
> 16 *The twenty-four elders sitting on their thrones before God fell with their faces to the ground and worshiped him.*
> 17 *And they said, "We give thanks to you, Lord God, the Almighty, the one who is and who always was, for now you have assumed your great power and have begun to reign.*
> 18 *The nations were filled with wrath,*
> *but now the time of your wrath has come.*
> *It is time to judge the dead and reward your servants the prophets, as well as your holy people, and all who fear your name, from the least to the greatest.*
> *It is time to destroy all who have caused destruction on the earth."*
> 19 *Then, in heaven, the Temple of God was opened and the Ark of his covenant could be seen inside the Temple. Lightning flashed, thunder crashed and roared, and there was an earthquake and a terrible hailstorm."*

Christ will assume His role as Lord of all creation... finally! He will begin to reign and everything worldwide will be set right! The evildoers will be gone. Humanity will be saved! No more maddening deception! No more tyranny! No more lack! No more chronic illnesses! No more wars!

Praise the LORD!

35. Since the beginning of time, Christ, the King of the world, has not assumed His full position as King of the world. Who was allowed to rule as the rpince of the power of the air, acccording to Ephesians 2:2?

> Ephesians 2
> 2 *"You used to live in sin, just like the rest of the world, obeying the devil—the commander of the powers in the unseen world. He is the spirit at work in the hearts of those who refuse to obey God."*

the devil.

36. According to Revelation 11:18 above, what are the first things Christ will do when He assumes His power and begins to rule the world?

"It is time to judge the dead and reward your servants the prophets, as well as your holy people,

and all who fear your name, from the least to the greatest. It is time to destroy all who have caused destruction on the earth."

SUMMARY

John, an apostle, is charged with guiding and protecting God's people and the worship of the Lord. John is being shown that God's people will be trodden down, and the worship of the Lord will be devastated for a very long time, which will cause God's people to grieve in sackcloth. 42 months = 1260 days = 3 ½ years = Time, Times, and Half a Time = Period of Striving/Battle = Jupiter / Melchizedek loop.

But the Lord established two institutions that are intended for the protection of the righteous and judgment on evildoers. These institutions have been given authority to mete out justice and punish evildoers. One institution is represented by Elijah who shut the heavens so the sky would not rain. Elijah represents the prophets / religion. The other institution is represented by the one who turned water to blood, Moses, who represents the law/government. At some point, the witnesses "finish their testimony," which means they stop fulfilling their duties to protect the righteous and punish the wicked. Then they are "killed," symbolically. This means that they will not be able to perform their duties because they will be so heavily infiltrated by the beast's minions. The government and religious institutions will still appear to be functioning.

Why did the beast not shut down the government and the religious institutions? The enemy knew we would wake up if there were no government and no religious institutions at all. So it has appeared that we have had an operating "church and state", but we haven't! The lawless ones have been running the law! The earth-dweller demons rejoiced because they were able to get away with their crimes, since the Church and the State were not fulfilling their roles in the earth.

But then a miracle happens! Revelation 11:11 says that "after 3 1/2 days the spirit of life from God entered them"! The Great Awakening! The true Church and State, which is God's people who are destined to rule and reign on earth, stood on their feet because the Spirit of the Lord entered them! The criminals are panicking in great fear! God's true Church and State are being raised up to positions of authority, and the enemy cannot stop it!

We are soon to witness an earthquake to bring down the lawless criminal network that has been running the Church and the State!

Now you know why they had to lie to us about the Two Witnesses!!! They couldn't let that truth get out!

15-HEAVENLY SIGN OF THE SON OF MAN

"End Times and 1000 Years of Peace" Chapter 13
Revelation 12

Here it is, folks! This is the chapter that will settle in your heart and mind that we are witnessing the End Times destruction of the Beast NWO that has wreaked so much havoc on the earth. How do I know for sure? Because the LORD gave us a beautiful heavenly clock. And He set an alarm. That alarm went off on September 23, 2017 and was the kickoff to the Great Awakening and the Battle of Armageddon. That explains everything we have experienced for the past several years. And this chapter will keep you encouraged and fighting until we cross the finish line! Ready to see for yourself? Let's Go!

1. Why did the LORD put the sun, moon, and stars in the heavens?

> Genesis 1
> *14 "And God said, Let there be lights in the firmament of the heaven to divide the day from the night; and let them be for **signs, and for seasons, and for days, and years.**" (KJV)*

For signs for us, as well as for seasons and day and years. He gives us signs through the stars...

His heavenly storybook.

2. The lights in the heavens mark seasons and days and years on the calendar, but what else?

Signs from the LORD.

3. Name a famous star sign in the Bible. (Hint- Christmas)

The Bethlehem Star.

4. Give one reason the LORD numbers the stars and give them all a name.

> Psalm 147

4 "He counts the stars and calls them all by name."

To help us understand the messages He is sending to us.

5. How are the heavens speaking messages to us from the LORD?

Psalm 19
1 "The heavens declare the glory of God; and the firmament show his handiwork.
2 Day unto day utters speech, and night unto night shows knowledge.
3 There is no speech nor language, where their voice is not heard.
4 Their line is gone out through all the earth, and their words to the end of the world. In them hath he set a tabernacle for the sun." (NKJV)

The LORD gives us knowledge through the stars, day after day after day. Everyone worldwide can see them. The "wandering stars" move through the constellations and each has an established Biblical meaning.

Do most know how to read the signs?

No. This information has been hidden.

6. What is the difference between Biblical Astronomy and Astrology/Horoscopes?

Biblical Astronomy is based on the Biblical meanings of the stars and the constellations, and the LORD speaking to us through the promises in His Word. Astrology and Horoscopes is about stars controlling humanity as if they had power and knowledge separate from the LORD.

7. Identify the five elements of this heavenly wonder.

Revelation 12
1 "Then I witnessed in heaven an event of great significance. I saw a woman clothed with the sun, with the moon beneath her feet, and a crown of twelve stars on her head.
2 She was pregnant, and she cried out because of her labor pains and the agony of giving birth."

This is the actual sign in the heavens described in Revelation 12.

Element 1 – **Virgo is the Woman. We know that be cause there are no other female major constellations through which the sun, moon, and stars appear.**

Element 2 – **The sun is bathing Virgo in light, right on her shoulder.**

Element 3 – *The moon is under her feet.*

Element 4 – *Twelve stars appeared above Virgo's head.*

Element 5 – *Jupiter enters Virgo's "womb" on the day President Trump was elected, and completed a loop over a 42-week gestation period.*

8. What is the Biblical name of the Zodiac?

Mazzaroth.

9. Three constellations are women – Virgo (the Virgin Bride of Christ), Andromeda (the Chained Woman/Church), and Cassiopeia (the Queen of Heaven.)
Which constellation is used in this Revelation 12:1-2 sign? How do we know?

The sun, moon, and stars do not appear in Andromeda or Cassiopeia because they are not on the elliptical path.

10. How is Virgo "clothed with" or "bathed in" the sun? *The sunlight is on her shoulder. This sign was actually not visible because it appeared during the season when Virgo is in daylight sky. We are able to see the formation on the Stellarium online planetarium.*

11. What might the sunlight symbolize?
Light of God's Goodness. Holiness and purity. Hope.

12. What might it mean that the moon is under Virgo's feet?

The moon many times represents the dark forces. The NWO will be crushed by the Great Awakening.

13. What 12 stars make up Virgo's crown?
Nine stars are in the Leo constellation plus three more stars, Mercury, Mars, Venus, lined up on September 23, 2017 to form Virgo's crown.

14. Which wandering star "travails" (does a loop) in Virgo's womb for 42 weeks?

Jupiter.

(Some stars stay in a constant location (constellation), while others move, doing loops and waves.)

15. What is that star's Biblical name and its meaning? (this means eternal King and Priest)

Jupiter's Biblical name is Melchizedek which means the eternal King and Priest, our LORD JESUS! This is the Christ star!

16. What is the significance of 42 weeks?

It is a 42-week is a gestation period. So this sign represents the birth of the Millennial Kingdom!

17. Did our LORD Jesus tell us to watch for a sign?

Yes.

18. What did our LORD Jesus call that sign and what did He say would happen exactly?

> Matthew 24
> *30 "And then shall appear the sign of the Son of man in heaven: and then shall all the tribes of the earth mourn, and they shall see the Son of man coming in the clouds of heaven with power and great glory. 31 And he shall send his angels with a great sound of a trumpet, and they shall gather together his elect from the four winds, from one end of heaven to the other."(KJV)*

Jesus called this sign the "Sign of the Son of Man."

He said when that sign appears three things would happen.

All the tribes on earth would mourn.

The Son of Man would come in power.

And He would send His angels to gather His chosen ones to fight.

Memorize each of the three elements of Matthew 24:30-31. This is VERY IMPORTANT.

19. What does "the Son of Man will come in the clouds of heaven with power" suggest?

Jesus will come into power to rule the earth!

20. What does "then shall all of the tribes of the earth mourn" suggest?

Awakening to the knowledge of the NWO's crimes against humanity will break our hearts, and the Battle of Armageddon will cause a lot of division and sadness, and some won't make it through.

21. What does "the gathering His elect from the four corners" suggest?

The angels awakened warriors from all over the world to fight in the digital Battle of Armageddon.

22. Search "Woman in Labor" on *BibleGateway.com* and write three Bible verses with this phrase. What happens when the "woman in labor" appears?

"They were gripped with terror and writhed in pain like a woman in labor." (Psalm 48:6)

"and people are terrified. Pangs of anguish grip them, like those of a woman in labor. They look helplessly at one another, their faces aflame with fear." (Isaiah 13:8)

"Do men give birth to babies? Then why do they stand there, ashen-faced, hands pressed against their sides like a woman in labor?" (Jeremiah 30:6)

23. Do you think the "Woman in Labor" is the name in the Old Testament for the "Sign of the Son of Man"? Why or Why Not?

Yes. I believe the "Sign of the Son of Man" is the "Woman in Labor" talked about eighteen times in the Old Testament because both talk about giving birth, and they both talk about intense reactions from the people, some mourning and some panicking, just as we are witnessing.

24. Read about the second wonder (heavenly sign) in Revelation 12.

> Revelation 12
> 3 "Then I witnessed in heaven another significant event. I saw a large red dragon with seven heads and ten horns, with seven crowns on his heads.
> 4 His tail swept away one-third of the stars in the sky, and he threw them to the earth. He stood in front of the woman as she was about to give birth, ready to devour her baby as soon as it was born.
> 5 She gave birth to a son who was to rule all nations with an iron rod. And her child was snatched away from the dragon and was caught up to God and to his throne."

How does this passage compare with the Draco constellation?

Draco has a long tail and gives us an image of satan and the fallen angels (1/3 of the stars symbolically) being cast out of heaven.

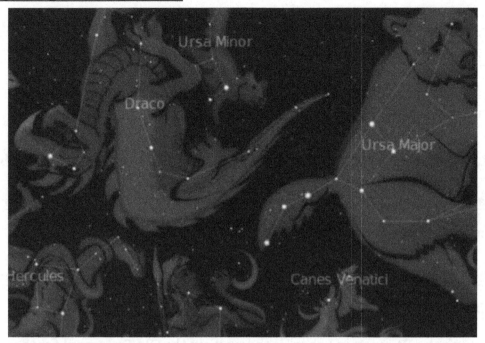

25. How does this passage compare with the Ophiuchus/Serpens constellation?

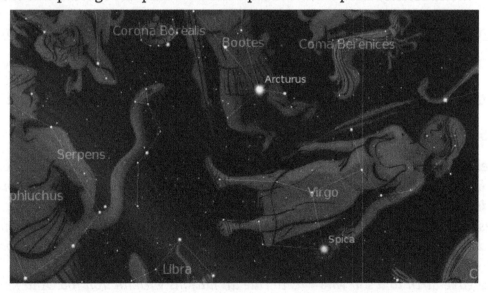

The Serpens constellation gives us the image found in the second part of Revelation 12:14, where "he stood in front of the woman as she was about to give birth, ready to devour her baby as soon as it was born." The enemy is constantly ready to strike to stop the Millennial Kingdom of Christ.

26. Based on these constellations the LORD put in the heavens, what does the great dragon represent? (Also see Revelation 20:2 for a hint.)

satan.

27. "*I saw a large red dragon with seven heads and ten horns, with seven crowns on his heads.*" No matter what the heads, horns, and crowns specifically represent, what does this awful wonder represent?

Satanic authority on earth

28. What does **Head** of State indicate? *Authority – The dragon has seven heads as in complete authority!*

29. What does **Horns** on a bull indicate? *Raw power – The dragon has ten horns to destroy.*

30. What does a **Crown** indicate? *Royalty – The dragon believes he has the right to rule earth.*

31. What does "his tail drew **the third part** of the stars of heaven and cast them to earth" remind you of? (1/3 = 33%)

Draco's tail gives us an image of satan and 33% of the fallen angels being cast out of heaven.

That connects us to the 33 degree Secret Societies who are their minions.

32. "*The dragon stood before the woman to devour her child as soon as it was born.*" (Revelation 12:4) Clearly this verse depicts satan's bloodthirsty cannibalistic nature – also known as Baal worship. It also shows that the dragon is determined to prevent the Kingdom of Christ from being established on earth.
How does verse 5 show the inevitability of Christ assuming His Kingly authority on earth?

> Revelation 12
> 5 "*She gave birth to a son who was to rule all nations with an iron rod. And her child was snatched away from the dragon and was caught up to God and to his throne.*"

Christ will rule the wicked with an iron rod! He will be in charge whether they like it or not!

33. The woman in Revelation 12:6 is not speaking specifically about the Virgin Mary. Who does the woman represent?

> Revelation 12
> 6 "*And the woman fled into the wilderness, where God had prepared a place to care for her for 1,260 days.*

7 Then there was war in heaven. Michael and his angels fought against the dragon and his angels.
8 And the dragon lost the battle, and he and his angels were forced out of heaven.
9 This great dragon—the ancient serpent called the devil, or Satan, the one deceiving the whole world—was thrown down to the earth with all his angels."

The Bride of Christ – those who love Him.

34. 1260 days = __*42*__ months = *3 ½* Years = Time, Times, and *Half a Time.*
These numbers all equal the circuit of Jupiter/Melchizedek. And it appears to represent a time of battle/struggle to take the Kingdom by force.

35. In Revelation 12:7 there is an epic battle between __*Michael*__ and his holy angels vs. *the dragon* and his fallen angels. In that battle, the great dragon and his fallen angels were cast out of "heaven" to "earth." Do you think verse 7 is talking about literal heaven, or positions of authority?

Positions of authority on earth.

36. Let's focus our attention on Revelation 12:10-12.

> Revelation 12
> *10 "Then I heard a loud voice shouting across the heavens,*
> *"It has come at last— salvation and power*
> *and the Kingdom of our God, and the authority of his Christ.*
> *For the accuser of our brothers and sisters*
> *has been thrown down to earth—*
> *the one who accuses them before our God day and night.*
> *11 And they have defeated him by the blood of the Lamband by their testimony.*
> *And they did not love their lives so much*
> *that they were afraid to die.*
> *12 Therefore, rejoice, O heavens!*
> *And you who live in the heavens, rejoice!*
> *But terror will come on the earth and the sea,*
> *for the devil has come down to you in great anger,*
> *knowing that he has little time."*

Fill in the blanks of Revelation 12:10 and just imagine the joy when this happens!

It has come at last - *Salvation*, and *Power*, and the *Kingdom* of our God, and the power of His Christ have come, for the accuser of our brethren has been cast down. What does this verse indicate happens to the earthly authority of the dragon?

All satanic authority is removed from earth. That is so hard to imagine, but it will happen!

37. How do God's people defeat satan? (see Revelation 12:11)

We defeat the enemy by the blood of the Lamb and by our testimony.

38. How do we win by the blood of the Lamb? (see Revelation 12:11) *First, our sins are forgiven by the blood of Christ and we stand blameless, giving us the power of His righteous Spirit within us.*

39. How do we win by the word of our testimony? (Revelation 12:11) *Since we have the Spirit of the LORD working within us and guiding us into all truth, we can testify to the truth every day on every subject!*

40. What do we not fear? (Revelation 12:11) *death.*

41. Currently the battle still rages on. The evildoers are panicking. See verse 12.

For the devil has come down to you, having great *anger*

because he knows he has *little time.*

That explains why there is so much persecution...to silence the trumpeters in a last ditch desperate effort to regain control. (Revelation 12:12)

42. Who might this eagle represent in Revelation 12:13-14? How is the woman kept safe?

> Revelation 12
> *13 "When the dragon realized that he had been thrown down to the earth, he pursued the woman who had given birth to the male child.*
> *14 But she was given two wings like those of a great eagle so she could fly to the place prepared for her in the wilderness. There she would be cared for and protected from the dragon for a time, times, and half a time."*

The eagle might represent America, as the wings in Daniel 7:4 did. America is destined to rescue the world. Everything that is happening is intended to keep humanity as safe as possible, while defeating the dark forces. This war is REAL.

43. Revelation 12:15-16 is surely symbolic. How could this flood from the dragon's mouth carry us away, and how could that flood be swallowed up? (Remember this is an

INFORMATION WAR with Flood of Deception.)

> Revelation 12
> *15 "Then the dragon tried to drown the woman with a flood of water that flowed from his mouth. 16 But the earth helped her by opening its mouth and swallowing the river that gushed out from the mouth of the dragon."*

Whenever the NWO spews their lies, patriots expose the truth, swallowing up their lies so they have no negative effect on us, like they used to. It just exposes the NWO even more!

44. Notice that instead of the dragon creating both sides of proxy wars that end up killing humanity, this war is real war <u>between the dragon and the righteous.</u> What are the identifying characteristics of woman's offspring?

> Revelation 12
> *17 "And the dragon was angry at the woman and declared war against the rest of her children—all who keep God's commandments and maintain their testimony for Jesus. 18 Then the dragon took his stand on the shore beside the sea."*

They keep God's commandments and maintain our testimony for Jesus. Patriots aren't fake Christians. We follow God and want the earth to be filled with justice and peace for everybody!

45. Based on the heavenly star sign, what has humanity been experiencing since September 23, 2017?
The Great Awakening and the ***Battle of Armageddon.***

46. Do you believe our victory is inevitable? Soon? Why? Why not?

Yes! I believe so because President Trump said 2024 is our final battle! And all the prophecies lead us to believe the Battle of Armageddon started September 23, 2017 with the Sign of the Son of Man, and we are nearing its completion!

The next study guide topic is about two terrible beasts and the "Mark of the Beast." Don't worry! Just be prepared to think very differently from what Hollywood and the mainstream church lead us to believe. Since you are awake now, you will know this interpretation is the truth!

16-HIDEOUS BEASTS & MARK OF THE BEAST

"End Times and 1000 Years of Peace" Chapter 14 & 15
Revelation 13

Buckle up for Study Guide 16 because it's coming in hot! We will study the two Beasts of Revelation and the Mark of the Beast! This is not for the faint of heart! Never fear! The LORD is here!

1. The beast described in Revelation 13:1 comes out of the sea. What does the sea usually symbolize?

> Revelation 13
> 1 *"Then I saw a beast rising up out of the sea. It had seven heads and ten horns, with ten crowns on its horns. And written on each head were names that blasphemed God."*

Humanity – so the beast is humans who are under the power of demons.

2. How might this beast "from the sea" described in Revelation 13:1 give us a clue about how the New World Order has enslaved humanity?

The NWO tricked us into being under the "Law of the Sea," under which we are considered as chattel, so our God-given rights are stripped away.

3. Write your thoughts on the symbolism of the seven heads.

Seven heads symbolizes complete authority!

4. Write your thoughts on the symbolism of the 10 horns.

The ten horns symbolize raw power to destroy.

5. Write your thoughts on the symbolism of the 10 crowns.

The ten crowns symbolize the royalty right to rule. The beast has usurped this right which belongs to Christ alone.

> Revelation 13
> *2 "This beast looked like a leopard, but it had the feet of a bear and the mouth of a lion! And the dragon gave the beast his own power and throne and great authority."*

6. Compare the symbolism in Revelation 13:2 with Daniel 7.

> Daniel 7
> *3 "Then four huge beasts came up out of the water, each different from the others.*
> *4 The first beast was like a lion with eagles' wings. As I watched, its wings were pulled off, and it was left standing with its two hind feet on the ground, like a human being. And it was given a human mind.*
>
> *5 Then I saw a second beast, and it looked like a bear. It was rearing up on one side, and it had three ribs in its mouth between its teeth. And I heard a voice saying to it, "Get up! Devour the flesh of many people!"*
>
> *6 Then the third of these strange beasts appeared, and it looked like a leopard. It had four bird's wings on its back, and it had four heads. Great authority was given to this beast.*
>
> *7 Then in my vision that night, I saw a fourth beast—terrifying, dreadful, and very strong. It devoured and crushed its victims with huge iron teeth and trampled their remains beneath its feet. It was different from any of the other beasts, and it had ten horns."*

The beast in Revelation 13:2 is a combination of a leopard, with the feet of a bear and the mouth of a lion, given authority from the dragon! Daniel 7 has three separate beasts – a lion, a bear, and a leopard, and the fourth beast has ten horns and is dreadful and devouring.

7. How might Revelation 13:3 have been fulfilled already?

> Revelation 13
> *3 "I saw that one of the heads of the beast seemed wounded beyond recovery—but the fatal wound was healed! The whole world marveled at this miracle and gave allegiance to the beast."*

Very likely this passage was fulfilled after WW2, when the Nazi regime was supposedly destroyed, but ended up proliferating and infiltrating governments all around the world.

8. Clearly from Revelation 13:4-5 this beast has great power and influence that most do not believe can be overcome, humanly speaking. This beast speaks great things and blasphemies. What does that indicate?

Revelation 13

4 "They worshiped the dragon for giving the beast such power, and they also worshiped the beast. "Who is as great as the beast?" they exclaimed. "Who is able to fight against him?"
5 Then the beast was allowed to speak great blasphemies against God. And he was given authority to do whatever he wanted for forty-two months."

After the Nazi regime escaped justice and gained control of governments and organizations worldwide, many joined them, thinking if an entire world war could not stop them, then no one could! The NWO has been able to do whatever they wanted and waged war on humanity.

9. Again we see a period of battle for 42 months. (see Revelation 13:5) Comparing all the times 42 months is used in Scripture, what do you deduce?

Every time 42 months, 3 ½ years, 1260 days, and Time, Times, and Half a Times is used in Scripture, it is referring to a about a period of battle.

10. The beast blasphemes/curses God. When Revelation 13:6 says the beast blasphemes *"those who dwell in heaven"* who is he talking about? (See Ephesians 2:6 *"And hath raised us up together, and made us sit together in heavenly places in Christ Jesus."*)

Revelation 13

6 "And he spoke terrible words of blasphemy against God, slandering his name and his dwelling—that is, those who dwell in heaven."

The enemy hates God and hates those who love and follow God. "Those who dwell in heaven" refers to those who love and follow God.

11. Revelation 13:7 says the beast overcomes the saints, so he has had power over all of humanity.

Revelation 13

7 "And the beast was allowed to wage war against God's holy people and to conquer them. And he was given authority to rule over every tribe and people and language and nation."

Compare this verse to:

Daniel 8

25 "He will be a master of deception and will become arrogant; he will destroy many without warning. He will even take on the Prince of princes in battle, but he will be broken, though not by human power."

Is there hope? What promise in Daniel 8:25 gives us hope?

It appears, humanly speaking, that there is no way to extricate ourselves from the NWO

AntiChrist system. But God promises in His Holy Word that the enemy will be broken, though not

by human power. The LORD Himself will rescue us!

12. Who actually WORSHIPS the beast? (worship as in obey, follow, give themselves over to)

> Revelation 13
> *8 "And all the people who belong to this world worshiped the beast. They are the ones whose names were not written in the Book of Life that belongs to the Lamb who was slaughtered before the world was made."*

All who belong to this world, whose name are not written in the Book of Life, are those who do

satan's bidding. That is not talking about people of a different religion. The LORD sees through

all of that down to the actions and the motives of the heart. (see Hebrews 4:12)

13. Many times our LORD Jesus would say, "If any man has ears to hear, let him hear." Many are too brainwashed to understand. Jesus is coming to save the brainwashed too. How can that phrase help Patriots in this battle as we try to redpill people?

> Revelation 13
> *9 "Anyone with ears to hear should listen and understand."*

We do not have the responsibility of changing someone's heart or mind. Our responsibility is to

share the truth, and leave the rest to the LORD.

14. Put Revelation 13:10 in your own words.

> Revelation 13
> *10 "Anyone who is destined for prison will be taken to prison. Anyone destined to die by the sword will die by the sword. This means that God's holy people must endure persecution patiently and remain faithful."*

We are in a real war. We must keep fighting and wait for God's perfect timing on ending this very

real war. Each of us has a destiny in God's hands, which will be fulfilled.

(Reminder – our battle is NOT against flesh and blood, with guns and bullets, but against demonic forces.)

15. The second beast comes out of the earth. Two horns like a lamb. Spoke like a dragon. Who is this?

Revelation 13

11 "Then I saw another beast come up out of the earth. He had two horns like those of a lamb, but he spoke with the voice of a dragon."

The second beast is primarily the religious institutions.

16. The second beast has the same satanic power but is not intending to rule the earth. The second beast causes those on earth to worship the first beast. Give examples of how they do this.

Revelation 13

12 "He exercised all the authority of the first beast. And he required all the earth and its people to worship the first beast, whose fatal wound had been healed."

They appear innocent and trustworthy like a lamb, but they are not working for the benefit of the people, but for themselves and the NWO satanic (dragon) AntiChrist. They keep the religious groups fighting each other, rather than fighting the cabal. They confuse people about End Times to keep them from identifying the real enemy. They mislead people and burden them with guilt so they don't feel close to God. They turn a blind eye to true wickedness, urging forgiveness, to prevent people from working for justice on earth. They lead people to obey the government no matter what ridiculous laws they make, like mask mandates.

17. Give examples of how the second beast makes "fire come down from heaven" to deceive humanity into following the beast.

Revelation 13

13 "He did astounding miracles, even making fire flash down to earth from the sky while everyone was watching.

14 And with all the miracles he was allowed to perform on behalf of the first beast, he deceived all the people who belong to this world. He ordered the people to make a great statue of the first beast, who was fatally wounded and then came back to life."

At the upper levels of the religious institutions, they work in Secret Societies to orchestrate division among the people, and obedience to the government. This all appears to happen naturally, but it is orchestrated to control the masses and keep anyone from rising up against the AntiChrist system. For example, almost all the churches obeyed the Covid lockdowns and mask mandate and vaccine requirements, as if they made the choice independently. But it was

orchestrated from the top.

18. How might the second beast "give life" to the image of the first beast? To speak and to kill?

Think Fake News and modern technology.

> Revelation 13
> 15 "He was then permitted to give life to this statue so that it could speak. Then the statue of the beast commanded that anyone refusing to worship it must die."

John might have seen an actual TV screen, which looked like a talking statue to him! Whether he did or not, the second beast religious institutions have enforced compliance, as if they were told to by a miracle or God Himself!

19. The "Mark of the Beast" is likely the part of the Book of Revelation and End Times teaching that is used most to trick the people.

> Revelation 13
> 16 "He required everyone—small and great, rich and poor, free and slave—to be given a mark on the right hand or on the forehead.
> 17 And no one could buy or sell anything without that mark, which was either the name of the beast or the number representing his name."

Try to forget everything you've heard about the Mark of the Beast. Then write in your own words what would be the "mark" or the "identifying aspect" of the beast/satanic cabal.

This "mark" is given to all kinds of people when they join the NWO team. With that mark, they have whatever they want. Without that mark, you are on the outside. Canceled. That makes life difficult for the outsiders. But the mark comes with a price, and they have to pay by doing the NWO's evil bidding.

If you wrote down pure evil, you're on the right track.

20. What is the most evil thing a human could do? Think demonic and think worldwide.

Traffick and harm children.

21. Would the New World Order cabal have a reason to deceive us about the meaning of "the Mark of the Beast?" How could that benefit the cabal?

Yes. They don't want anyone to identify them individually, or to identify the NWO Secret Society AntiChrist system.

22. Would the New World Order cabal allow the true meaning of the Mark of the Beast to be broadcast in Hollywood movies and in the mainstream church?

No way. That is TOP Secret.

23. Those who receive the Mark of the Beast are punished with eternal damnation. (Revelation 14:9-10) Do you think the LORD would the punish someone in eternal hell for taking an RFID chip under their skin, or a tattoo or vaccine, coerced or not?

No. The LORD would never do that. It is blasphemous to say He would.

24. Revelation 13:16 is not indicating that every man, woman, and child worships the Beast. But that ALL TYPES of people do. What TYPES of people swear allegiance to the first Beast?

> Revelation 13
> *16 "He required everyone—small and great, rich and poor, free and slave—to be given a mark on the right hand or on the forehead."*

Small, Great, Rich, Poor, Free, Slave. Because joining is about the HEART, not any status.

25. Is the Mark of the Beast likely a physical mark? What do hands symbolize? What do foreheads represent? So what symbolically does it mean to receive a Mark of the Beast in their right hand or in their forehead?

No. The mark is not a physical mark, even though some might get a tattoo to show their allegiance to the NWO AntiChrist. Hands symbolize actions. Foreheads symbolize intentions and thoughts and words. They swear allegiance of their actions, intentions, thoughts, and words to the NWO.

26. Can someone be forced to take the Mark of the Beast under coercion? Unknowingly? Why or Why not?

No. Because to take the Mark of the Beast is to surrender the will to the demons.

27. How does someone "take" the Mark of the Beast? (think the mark of pure evil/satanic/evil rituals)

By doing something evil. Think hazing to the extreme. The Secret Society wants to know they can trust you to do evil for them.

28. What is the cabal's reward for those who take the Mark of the Beast? Give examples.

> Revelation 13

17 "And no one could buy or sell anything without that mark, which was either the name of the beast or the number representing his name."

They get wealth and power and prestige. They are promoted in the media and protected from criminal prosecution.

29. Revelation 13:18 is the verse about the number 666.

Revelation 13
18 "Wisdom is needed here. Let the one with understanding solve the meaning of the number of the beast, for it is the number of a man. His number is 666."

The verse says "wisdom is needed" to understand the meaning of 666. Is it likely that popular cultural, Hollywood, or modern theology would accurately define the meaning of 666?

No. Popular culture, Hollywood, and modern theology are the ones keeping this truth hidden!

30. *"It is the number of a man."* How is 666 the number of man? (See Revelation 13:18) (Hint Adam, Day of creation, Body/Soul/Spirit)

Man was created on the 6th day and is a tripartite being of body, soul, and spirit.

31. *"The number of the beast"* is 666. How is 666 also the number of the Beast? (13:18)

The Beast AntiChrist uses the number 666 as their rallying cry to attack those who follow God.

32. How does the New World Order use the 666 symbolism? Give examples.

They use 666 symbolism to help people identify their attack techniques. These are a few groups that use 666 in their logos: Disney, Cern, Chrome, Monster, Kleenex, Kellogg's, and Adobe.

33. Revelation 13 describes two beasts....one from the sea and one from the earth. These beasts are clearly simultaneous and work together with satanic power to rule humanity. Those who join forces with them are greatly rewarded. What are your thoughts about this chapter?

This information helps make sense of how the AntiChrist system has worked in a highly organized way to attack humanity. Now that we know who we are fighting, and it's not each other, we can focus our efforts on destroying them!

17-144,000 AND TWO HARVESTS

"End Times and 1000 Years of Peace" Chapter 16
Revelation 14

If you love the stars - the Biblical signs the LORD put in the heavens - you will love Study Guide #17! We will also learn about the great Army of the Battle of Armageddon, and the Two Great Harvests! One Harvest of Judgment for the demon worshipers... and one Harvest of Blessings for humanity! Let's Go!

> Revelation 14
> 1 *"Then I saw the Lamb standing on Mount Zion, and with him were 144,000 who had his name and his Father's name written on their foreheads."*

1. Who does the Lamb symbolize? I know that's an easy one, but I'm reminding everyone that Revelation is filled with symbolism. Many modern interpretations of Revelation tend to forget that.

__The Lamb represents Jesus. Of course. He's standing on the Mountain of the City of God, which is__

__symbolism for having the highest place of authority.__

2. Who are the 144,000? Is this a symbolic number? (See Revelation 7:4–8)

__The chosen warriors for the Battle of Armageddon. Symbolic of 12,000 warriors from each__

__tribe.__

3. List the 12 tribes of Israel. (see Revelation 7:4-8) (NOTE: Ephraim and Manasseh, Joseph's 2 sons whom Jacob adopted, are not listed here.)

__Judah__   *__Manasseh__*

Reuben	_Simeon_
Gad	_Levi_
Asher	_Issachar_
Naphtali	_Zebulon_
Joseph	_Benjamin_

4. Are the 144,000 only from those who identify as Jews? See James 1. Explain.

> James 1
> 1 "This letter is from James, a slave of God and of the Lord Jesus Christ.
> I am writing to the "twelve tribes"—Jewish believers scattered abroad."

**Some might not identify themselves as Jews. Some people who are actually part of the scattered tribes of Israel since the Assyrian dispersion, might not know they are Israelites. Whether they are or not, they walk with God.**

5. The "_144,000 had his name and his Father's name written on their foreheads._" Their tribe name is not written in their foreheads. The 144,000 might not know they're from an Israelite tribe, or they might be a grafted in branch. What name **is** written in their foreheads and what does that indicate?

**Their Father's name is written on their forehead. They identify as a follower of God.**

6. Where are they standing?

**Next to Christ on Mount Zion.**

7. Does this indicate a physical location or symbolic location?___**Symbolic**_

8. What does Mount Zion symbolize?

**The City of God, and the highest place of authority.**

> Revelation 14
> 2 "And I heard a sound from heaven like the roar of mighty ocean waves or the rolling of loud thunder. It was like the sound of many harpists playing together.
> 3 This great choir sang a wonderful new song in front of the throne of God and before the four living beings and the twenty-four elders. No one could learn this song except the 144,000 who had been redeemed from the earth.
> 4 They have kept themselves as pure as virgins, following the Lamb wherever he goes. They have been purchased from among the people on the earth as a special offering (**the**

firstfruits) to God and to the Lamb. They have told no lies; they are without blame."

9. What is the mission of the Lamb and the 144,000? ***To expose and defeat the satanic criminal cabal, also known as the AntiChrist system.***

10. Do they hold weapons? ___no___

11. What are they doing in Revelation 14:2–3?

Singing praise to the LORD

12. Who are they singing before? (See Study Guide Chapter 7 - Revelation 4)

The throne of God, the four living beings and the 24 elders.

13. What does that indicate about God and His people? ***We are unified around the throne. The four living beings symbolize all those who love God from time immemorial.***

14. So, what is the primary weapon of the 144,000?

Praise and truth.

15. What do they sound like? ***A storm.***

16. What does it mean that only the 144,000 could learn that song?

Only those who have fought in the Battle of Armageddon know what battle has been like. We will have a camaraderie for all time that others won't be able to understand.

17. Are only physical virgins included in the 144,000? ***no.***

18. What does "pure as virgins" and "they follow the Lamb wherever He goes" indicate?

"Pure as virgins" means pure in our relationship with God. "Follow the Lamb" means we are willing to do whatever the LORD leads us to do to complete the assignment He has given us.

19. What does it mean that the 144,000 were redeemed from among men?

Hand-selected by God.

20. How does that coincide with being the firstfruits to God? (See Revelation 14:4)

The firstfruits are the first grains of the harvest season, and they are hand-picked for the omer bundle. We were the first to awaken and to be called to fight in the Battle of Armageddon.

(Hand-chosen like the omer in the omer bundle.)

21. What does firstfruits mean? (See 1 Corinthians Chapters 15:23 NKJV & 20 & Revelation 20:4–6.)

__Resurrection of our incorruptible bodies, as in Christ is the firstfruits – the First Resurrection.__

> Revelation 14
> *5 "They have told no lies; they are without blame."*

22. What does it mean "in their mouth was found no guile?" And "they are without fault before the throne of God?" (By the way, the modern church does not like us to consider ourselves blameless.)

__The 144,000 are not liars or deceivers. We are all about the truth!__

Here are more heavenly wonders! These are literally messages from the Lord to us through the stars.

23. Remember, the wandering stars Venus, Jupiter, Mercury, Saturn, and Mars give us messages. The LORD decoded these three for us here. Remember the three wandering stars in the Sign of the Son of Man? Which stars were they?

__Mercury, Mars, and Venus.__

FIRST ANGEL – MERCURY

It is likely that the three heavenly messengers in Revelation 14 represent the three wandering stars in the Sign of the Son of Man. Mercury is the first "angel/messenger" in the heaven (in far left circle). Mercury is giving this message to the earth-dwellers (the wicked) AND every nation, kindred, tongue and people. See Revelation 14:6

> Revelation 14
> *6 "And I saw another angel flying through the sky, carrying the eternal Good News to proclaim to the people who belong to this world—to every nation, tribe, language, and people.*
> *7 "Fear God," he shouted. "Give glory to him. For the time has come when he will sit as judge. Worship him who made the heavens, the earth, the sea, and all the springs of water."*

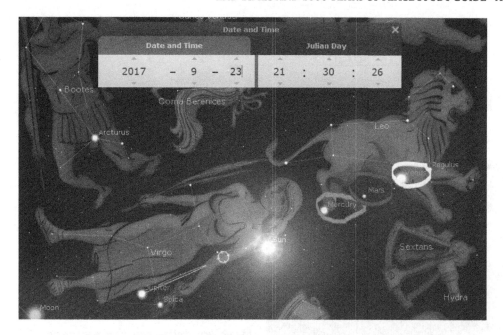

25. What is Mercury's message in Revelation 14:6?

"Fear God," he shouted. "Give glory to him. For the time has come when he will sit as judge. Worship him who made the heavens, the earth, the sea, and all the springs of water."

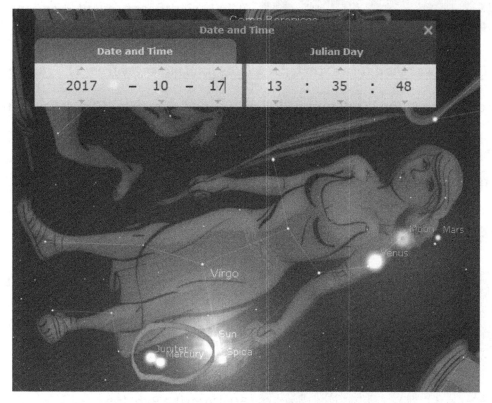

26. From whom did Mercury receive its message

and on what date?

__Jupiter/ Melchizedek on 10/30/2017__

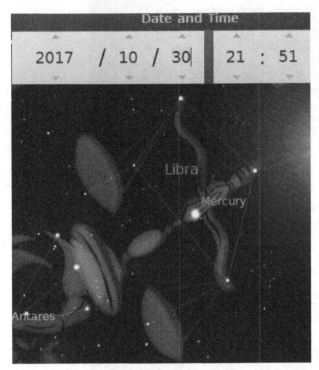

27. In which constellation was the Revelation 14:6 message delivered? What is the significance of the location where the message was delivered?

__Mercury delivered the message of judgment to the scales of justice! Perfect!__

28. On what date was the message delivered? What significant event happened on this date?

__10/30/2017 That was the date we started receiving intel messages from 17!! Justice!__

The Battle of Armageddon is following Biblical timing to precision! Trust the plan!

SECOND ANGEL – VENUS

Venus is the second "angel/messenger" in the heaven (in far right circle). (See Revelation 14:8)

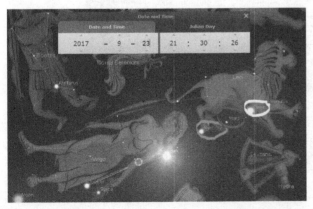

Revelation 14
8 *"Then another angel followed him through the sky, shouting, "Babylon is fallen—that great city is fallen—because she made all the nations of the world drink the wine of her passionate immorality."*

30. Describe Babylon.

__The New World Order city of evil including Beast, the False Prophet, the Harlot and satan.__

31. Why is Babylon under such judgment from God, per Revelation 14:8?

__Because she made all the nations of the world drink the wine of her passionate immorality.__

__Babylon forced the cup of evil on all the world, per Habakkuk 2.__

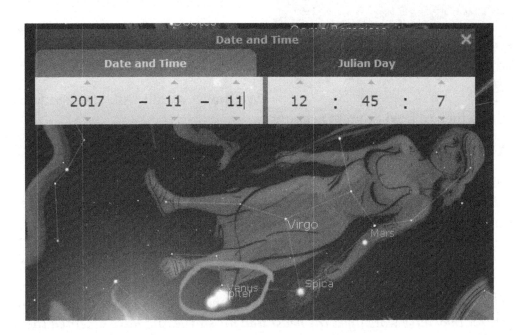

32. From whom did the second angel receive its message and on what date? What was the message?

__Jupiter/ Melchizedek on 11/11/2017__

__"Babylon is fallen—that great city is fallen—because she made all the nations of the world drink__

__the wine of her passionate immorality."__

33. In which constellation was the Revelation 14:8 message delivered? What does the location in the constellation indicate?

__In the pincers of Scorpio, symbolizing the LORD has the NWO in His clutches and they can't get__

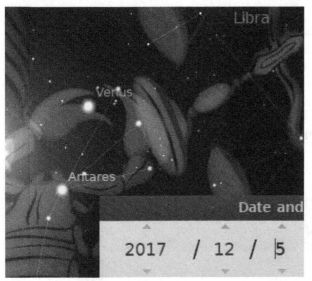

away.

34. On what date was the message delivered? What significant event happened on this date?

__12/5/2017 This was the date the keystone unlocked the door of all doors... exposing the data of all the secret Deep State messages proving their crimes against humanity.__

We have it all! All the evidence against Babylon with which to hold them to account!

THIRD ANGEL – MARS

Revelation 14

9 "Then a third angel followed them, shouting, "Anyone who worships the beast and his statue or who accepts his mark on the forehead or on the hand

10 must drink the wine of God's anger. It has been poured full strength into God's cup of wrath. And they will be tormented with fire and burning sulfur in the presence of the holy angels and the Lamb.

11 The smoke of their torment will rise forever and ever, and they will have no relief day or night, for they have worshiped the beast and his statue and have accepted the mark of his name."

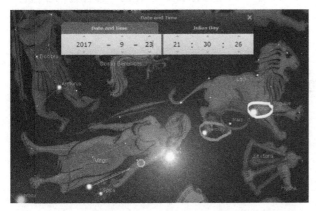

35. Mars is the third "angel/messenger" in the heaven (in middle circle). (See Revelation 14:9-11) What is the message of the third angel?

__"Anyone who worships the beast and his statue or who accepts his mark on the forehead or on the hand must drink the wine of God's anger... and be tormented day and night forever."__

36. From which star did the third angel receive its message and on what date? (Notice that Jupiter and Mars conjoin in Libra, the scales of justice.)

**Jupiter/ Melchizedek on 1/6/2018**

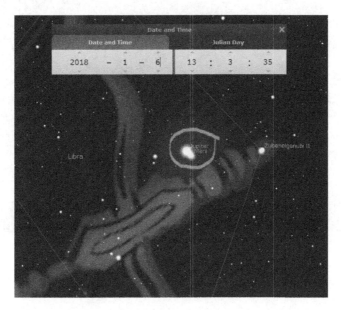

37. In which constellation was the Revelation 14:9-11 message delivered? What is the significance of the location where the message was delivered?

Ophiucus, the Serpent Wrestler. Ophiucus represents our LORD Jesus as the One who wrestles the NWO snake and will defeat them.

38. On what date was the message delivered? What significant event happened on this date?

3/18/2018. North Korea was set free from the NWO cabal CIA handlers! They can no longer be used to terrorize the world!

39. What is the identifying mark of these under God's judgment and what is that mark? (Revelation 14:11)

Those with the Mark of the Beast will suffer eternal torment under the wrath of Almighty God. Therefore we know this Mark is NOT a chip or a vaccine. The Mark of the Beast is KNOWINGLY SURRENDERING ONE'S WILL TO SATAN.

40. What punishment will they receive?

They will be in torment under the wrath of God.

41. How long is the punishment they receive?

__Day and night forever.__

> Revelation 14
> *12 "This means that God's holy people must endure persecution patiently, obeying his commands and maintaining their faith in Jesus.*
> *13 And I heard a voice from heaven saying, "Write this down: Blessed are those who die in the Lord from now on. Yes, says the Spirit, they are blessed indeed, for they will rest from their hard work; for their good deeds follow them!""*

42. But our future is vastly different, Patriots! We are the Blessed of the Lord! We can endure because our victory is sure! Read Revelation 4:12-14.

> Revelation 14
> *14 "Then I saw a white cloud, and seated on the cloud was someone like the Son of Man. He had a gold crown on his head and a sharp sickle in his hand."*

Who is the one who was seated on the white cloud in Revelation 14:14?

__Our LORD Jesus Christ, the King of the World!__

43. What does it mean that He sits on a cloud?

__He sits as the Highest Authority and power on earth__.

What does it mean that He is wearing a golden crown?

__He deserves the royal crown because He paid for the sins of humanity, and bought us back from the enemy.__

What does it mean that He is holding a sharp sickle?

__He has the power to harvest the believers and the power to harvest the grapes of wrath to judgment.__

> Revelation 14
> *15 "Then another angel came from the Temple and shouted to the one sitting on the cloud, "Swing the sickle, for the time of harvest has come; the crop on earth is ripe."*
> *16 So the one sitting on the cloud swung his sickle over the earth, and the whole earth was harvested.*
> *17 After that, another angel came from the Temple in heaven, and he also had a sharp sickle."*

44. What is the Lord harvesting in Revelation 14:15-17?

The grain – represent the Great Awakening of those who love God worldwide!

(The harvest is so great another angel comes to help reap!)

45. How are the two harvests "ripe?"

The harvest of grain are ripe to awaken and enjoy the Millennial Kingdom of Christ on earth.

The harvest of grapes are ripe for judgment!

46. What is our Lord Jesus initiating? He is the Lord of the Harvests!

He is initiating both harvests because He is the One who enabling both!

> Revelation 14
>
> 18 "Then another angel, who had power to destroy with fire, came from the altar. He shouted to the angel with the sharp sickle, "Swing your sickle now to gather the clusters of grapes from the vines of the earth, for they are ripe for judgment."
>
> 19 So the angel swung his sickle over the earth and loaded the grapes into the great winepress of God's wrath."

47. What is being harvested in Revelation 14:18-19? (notice this sickle is SHARP!)

The wicked who have joined in league with satan to destroy humanity are being eradicated!

48. Where does the angel come from? What does the angel say to the Lord?

This angel comes from the altar, where prayers have been made to save humanity. The angel says, "Swing your sickle now to gather the clusters of grapes from the vines of the earth, for they are ripe for judgment."

49. Where does the angel cast the grapes of wrath in Revelation 14:19?

Into the great winepress of God's wrath… in other words, into Hell.

50. Put Revelation 14:20 in your own words. Hint – it's symbolic!

> Revelation 14
>
> 20 "The grapes were trampled in the winepress outside the city, and blood flowed from the winepress in a stream about 180 miles long and as high as a horse's bridle."

The destruction of the NWO satanic criminal cabal will be a bloodbath! They will be destroyed to a level unimaginable. No one will miss it! Buckle up!

18-HEAVENLY SIGN OF GOD'S WRATH

"End Times and 1000 Years of Peace" Chapter 17
Revelation Chapter 15

Just like the plagues God sent on the Egyptians set the Israelites free, the LORD is using plagues to deliver us too! Revelation 15 shows us the seven final plagues in a beautiful heavenly sign.

Revelation 15
1 "Then I saw in heaven another marvelous event of great significance. Seven angels were holding the seven last plagues, which would bring God's wrath to completion."

1. Seven "angels" is another way to say seven messenger stars. Which constellation includes a small constellation of the seven stars?

 Taurus

2. What is the name of the small constellation of 7 stars? *Pleiades*

Also known as: ***The Seven Sisters***

3. How does this major constellation symbolize Christ?
Taurus symbolizes Christ coming on a rampage to destroy the wicked!

4. How does the smaller seven-star constellation symbolize those who love the LORD?

Pleiades represents the seven original churches in Revelation Chapters 2 and 3.

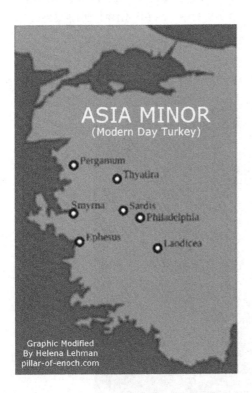

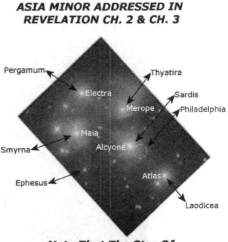

PLEIADES CORRELATION TO THE SEVEN CHURCHES IN ASIA MINOR ADDRESSED IN REVELATION CH. 2 & CH. 3

Note That The Star Of The Church Of Philadelphia, Which Is Given The Divine Promise That They Would ESCAPE The HOUR Of TRIAL In Rev. 3:10, Is Missing!

5. Where is the smaller constellation located inside the larger constellation, and what does that tell us about how the LORD feels about His followers?

Pleiades is tucked inside Jesus' heart, so they are loved and protected.

6. What song are the Patriots singing in Revelation 15:3-4, and how is it similar to the

struggle the Israelites experienced when they were delivered from Egypt?

> Revelation 15
>
> *2 "I saw before me what seemed to be a glass sea mixed with fire. And on it stood all the people who had been victorious over the beast and his statue and the number representing his name. They were all holding harps that God had given them.*
> *3 And they were singing the song of Moses, the servant of God, and the song of the Lamb:*
> *"Great and marvelous are your works, O Lord God, the Almighty.*
> *Just and true are your ways, O King of the nations.*
> *4 Who will not fear you, Lord, and glorify your name?*
> *For you alone are holy.*
> *All nations will come and worship before you,*
> *for your righteous deeds have been revealed.""*

Song: ***The Song of Moses***

Struggle: ***We are under a brutal, evil tyrannical government that is oppressing and destroying us.***

7. Why are they singing that song? ***Because they know only the LORD can deliver them. He is just.***

Even though humanly speaking, the cabal holds most of the positions of power, God's people know:

"Just and true are your ways, O King of the nations." The LORD is just and true and He is the King who can and will save us! (Revelation 15:3–4)

8. All the world will revere the LORD as the Holy One. Everyone will worship Him and know He has judged the wicked!

The Tabernacle of Testimony will be opened. What is the Tabernacle of Testimony / Ark of the Covenant / Mercy Seat? (For this next passage, remember how dangerous the Ark was in the "Raiders of the Lost Ark" movie.)

> Revelation 15
>
> *5 "Then I looked and saw that the Temple in heaven, God's Tabernacle, was thrown wide open.*
> *6 The seven angels who were holding the seven plagues came out of the Temple. They were clothed in spotless white linen with gold sashes across their chests."*
> *7 Then one of the four living beings handed each of the seven angels a gold bowl filled with*

the wrath of God, who lives forever and ever.

8 The Temple was filled with smoke from God's glory and power. No one could enter the Temple until the seven angels had completed pouring out the seven plagues."

The Tabernacle of Testimony / Ark of the Covenant is the place where God's Spirit dwelled in the Tabernacle. The blood of the sacrifice was offered on the Mercy Seat, and thereby the sins of the people were remitted.

9. What does the ark being opened / revealed indicate? Forgiveness and salvation have been available to everyone who repents, but the cabal refused to stop worshiping demons.

The Ark of the Covenant being opened signifies that forgiveness and salvation by the blood of Christ are available to everyone who repents of sin. Once God's judgment begins to fall, many repent. (Revelation 11:13) Also, it is possible that the blood that was discovered on the Ark of the Covenant will prove to the world who our Savior is. (see the Ark of the Covenant video on FreedomForce.LIVE)

10. Seven angels were coming out of the temple. Who gave the seven bowls of God's wrath to the angels in Revelation 15:7–8?

The four living beings.

11. Who are the golden bowls of God's wrath intended for?

The Beast AntiChrist NWO satanic cabal.

12. Who do the four living beings in Revelation 15:7 represent? (reminder the four living beings were also depicted in Revelation 4:6-9, 5:6-14, and 6:1-8.)

This is a diagram of the Israelite's encampment in the wilderness for 40 years.

The four sides of the encampment – North, South, East, and West – are depicted by the four living beings...a lion, a man, an ox, and an eagle, each of which symbolizes the four major tribes of Israel... which represents all the people who love God all over the world.

North - Eagle - Dan

South - Man - Reuben

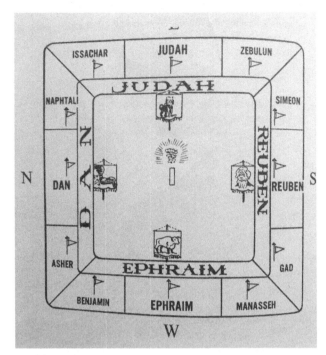

East - Lion - Judah

West - Ox - Ephraim

13. What is the significance of the four living beings having the bowls of God's wrath?

God's people have prayed for judgment to fall on the wicked and to be rescued, and their prayers are being answered!

14. What does it signify that the temple was filled with smoke from God's glory and power?

Let's take this opportunity to praise Him for His awesome power, which He is using to rescue humanity.

We Praise You LORD because Just and True are Your Ways! You are Holy! All the world will worship You as the King of the World. You deserve all the praise forever because of Your great love and power! We Praise You forever for making a way for our salvation, by Your own precious blood.

19-THE STORM

"End Times and 1000 Years of Peace" Chapter 18
Revelation Chapter 16

1. Who do you think the great voice out of the temple was who sent the seven angels to pour out the vials/bowls of God's wrath/judgment?

> Revelation 16
> *1 "Then I heard a mighty voice from the Temple say to the seven angels, "Go your ways and pour out on the earth the seven bowls containing God's wrath."*

<u>From His Temple of worship in Heaven, the LORD is finally initiating the destruction of the</u>

<u>wicked from the earth!</u>

Just a reminder from Revelation 5 and Revelation 8...the angels hold bowls of incense which symbolize our prayers for deliverance! Our prayers have filled the bowls to overflowing... and the LORD will answer our prayers to bring down judgment on the evildoers!

> Revelation 5
> *8 "And when he took the scroll, the four living beings and the twenty-four elders fell down before the Lamb. Each one had a harp, and **they held gold bowls filled with incense, <u>which are the prayers of God's people</u>.**"*

> Revelation 8
> *2 "I saw the seven angels who stand before God, and they were given seven trumpets.*
>
> *3 Then another angel with a gold incense burner came and stood at the altar. And a **<u>great amount of incense was given to him to mix with the prayers of God's people as an offering on the gold altar before the throne.</u>***
>
> ***<u>4 The smoke of the incense, mixed with the prayers of God's holy people,</u>** ascended up to God from the altar where the angel had poured them out."*

Now let's learn about the wrath and judgment of God that is inflicted on the NWO evildoers.

There might be several correct answers to the symbolism for each bowl. Our main focus is to remember that the wicked will receive signs of impending judgment, and then judgment upon judgment. Most of them will still refuse to repent, no matter what.

2. Remember from previous lessons, who are the ones who took the evil Mark of the Beast who are inflicted with the bowls of God's wrath?

> Revelation 16
> *2 "So the first angel left the Temple and poured out his bowl on the earth, and horrible, malignant sores broke out on everyone who had the mark of the beast and who worshiped his statue."*

The NWO satanic AntiChrist criminal cabal

3. What do you think the "noisome and grievous sores" might be? (Revelation 16:2)
NOTE: Always remember the Lord is rescuing humanity and bringing judgment on the demon worshipers.

These sores could be the physical effects of their horrifying rituals, and not getting the "fix" they

need. And it could be their utter shock and fear at realizing judgment is falling on them.

4. What could it mean that every living soul in the sea died?

> Revelation 16
> *3 "Then the second angel poured out his bowl on the sea, and it became like the blood of a corpse. And everything in the sea died."*

The sea many times represents commerce, so this could be the death to their financial empire, as

their assets are seized.

5. What could it mean that "rivers and fountains of water became blood?"

> Revelation 16
> *4 "Then the third angel poured out his bowl on the rivers and springs, and they became blood."*

This could represent that their happiness is gone and they don't even take pleasure in their evil

any more!

6. I love how the writer of the Revelation stops again and again to praise the LORD for bringing judgment on the evildoers and for rescuing humanity! Why do the angels and all of humanity concur that God's judgment is just?

> Revelation 16

5 "And I heard the angel who had authority over all water saying,
"You are just, O Holy One, who is and who always was,
because you have sent these judgments.

6 Since they shed the blood of your holy people and your prophets,
you have given them blood to drink.
It is their just reward."

7 And I heard a voice from the altar, saying,
"Yes, O Lord God, the Almighty, your judgments are true and just.""

"Since they shed the blood of your holy people and your prophets, you have given them blood to drink. It is their just reward."

7. What might "giving them blood to drink" in judgment symbolize? (Revelation 16:6)

They are having to drink down their own eternal death and judgment.

8. The fourth angel poured out God's judgment bowl on the scorching sun. What could that symbolize?

Revelation 16
8 "Then the fourth angel poured out his bowl on the sun, causing it to scorch everyone with its fire.
9 Everyone was burned by this blast of heat, and they cursed the name of God, who had control over all these plagues. They did not repent of their sins and turn to God and give him glory."

I think this is misery and overwhelming anger because everything they try to do to stop their

impending judgment fails!

9. What could the fifth angel's bowl indicate?

Revelation 16
10 "Then the fifth angel poured out his bowl on the throne of the beast, and his kingdom was plunged into darkness. His subjects ground their teeth in anguish."

This bowl could symbolize that the NWO power structure can no longer communicate covertly,

so they are having to do their operations in the "dark," but they get exposed anyway!

10. How do the demon worshipers respond to God's judgment falling on them?

Revelation 16
11 "and they cursed the God of heaven for their pains and sores. But they did not repent of their evil deeds and turn to God."

They curse God.

11. Do they repent of their evil deeds and turn to God? Why or why not? (Revelation 16:11)

They do not repent of their evil deeds and turn to God, because they can't. They can't get free from the demons who hold them captive. They don't want judgment, but they don't want God either.

12. Who do you think "the kings from the east" symbolize?

> Revelation 16
> *12 "Then the sixth angel poured out his bowl on the great Euphrates River, and it dried up so that the **kings from the east** could march their armies toward the west <u>without hindrance</u>."*

The royal kings who will rule and reign with Christ in the Millennial Kingdom! That's God's Army! They are exposing the NWO satan worshipers, and that knowledge really makes the cabal so angry!

13. What is the way of the kings of the east they are preparing? (Hint - the three wise men prepared for Christ's first advent.)

They are preparing for Christ to establish His Millennial Kingdom on earth!

14. In response to God's wrath being poured out of these vile creatures, even more evil comes pouring out of them! In concert they spew their evil vitriol against the LORD.

> Revelation 16
> *13 "And I saw three evil spirits that looked like frogs leap from the mouths of the dragon, the beast, and the false prophet."*

REMINDER: Who do these symbols represent?

Dragon - *satan.*

Beast - *New World Order.*

False Prophet - *Religious Institutions leaders who work with the NWO.*

15. What in Revelation 16:12 made the evil spirits get so angry in Revelation 16:13? Remember to mock them!

They are piping hot angry that Christ's Kingdom will be established on earth!

16. What did the unclean spirits do?

> Revelation 16
> *14 "For they are the spirits of devils, working miracles, which go forth unto the kings of the earth and of the whole world, to gather them to the battle of that great day of God Almighty."*

The demon spirits are so angry! They are in a fit rage to destroy God's people!

17. Where are the New World Order kings gathered to fight? Name the location and tell what that means symbolically. (Revelation 16:14)

Megiddo is the location and it means to expose, invade, and cut. But the Battle of Armageddon is being waged on the internet, not in a physical battlefield. This battle will expose, invade, and cut out the AntiChrist from the earth, and win over the hearts and minds of the brainwashed masses.

18. How is our Lord like a thief? Specifically at this point Jesus is asking this question at this climactic moment in history, when evildoers will be cast out of earth!

> Revelation 16
> *15 "Look, I will come as unexpectedly as a thief! Blessed are all who are watching for me, who keep their clothing ready so they will not have to walk around naked and ashamed."*

He's sneaky. You never know when He's going to surprise you with a word of encouragement, or some comfort or a bit of wisdom. He doesn't tell you He's coming with something great... He just surprises you unexpectedly, like a thief! But this passage is strange because in this verse He is literally fighting the Battle of Armageddon, but in the very next verse He says to watch for Him, because He will come as unexpectedly as a thief. As if He is leading the Battle, and people don't even see it.

19. How could our Lord Jesus' return be like a thief?

He could be on earth, and many not even realize it.

20. How does that square with "every will see Him?"

Possibly this could be that "every eye will see Him" but not every eye will recognize Him.

21. How should we watch for His return? What is the oil in our lamps? Where can we "buy" oil? (see the story of the wise and foolish virgins in Matthew 25:1-13)

> Matthew 25
> 1 "Then the Kingdom of Heaven will be like ten bridesmaids who took their lamps and went to meet the bridegroom.
> 2 Five of them were foolish, and five were wise.
> 3 The five who were foolish didn't take enough olive oil for their lamps,
> 4 but the other five were wise enough to take along extra oil.
> 5 When the bridegroom was delayed, they all became drowsy and fell asleep.
> 6 "At midnight they were roused by the shout, 'Look, the bridegroom is coming! Come out and meet him!'
> 7 "All the bridesmaids got up and prepared their lamps.
> 8 Then the five foolish ones asked the others, 'Please give us some of your oil because our lamps are going out.'
> 9 "But the others replied, 'We don't have enough for all of us. Go to a shop and buy some for yourselves.'
> 10 "But while they were gone to buy oil, the bridegroom came. Then those who were ready went in with him to the marriage feast, and the door was locked.
> 11 Later, when the other five bridesmaids returned, they stood outside, calling, 'Lord! Lord! Open the door for us!'
> 12 "But he called back, 'Believe me, I don't know you!'
> 13 "So you, too, must keep watch! For you do not know the day or hour of my return.""

We watch for His return by having oil in our lamps. This is not about being religious. It's about a spiritual connection with the LORD where we are listening for His voice. And we love to follow Him anywhere. The oil is the Spirit inside us, keeping the fires of love and devotion warm. The oil is replenished continually as we walk with Him.

22. How can we recognize our LORD? (See John 10:27)

> John 10
> 27 "My sheep listen to my voice; I know them, and they follow me."

We recognize His voice. We are accustomed to listening to Him and having Him guide us.

23. How will some who are not watching walk naked and ashamed like Revelation 16:15 says?

(See Zechariah 12:10-11 regarding the valley of Megiddo.)

Revelation 16

15 "Look, I will come as unexpectedly as a thief! Blessed are all who are watching for me, who keep their clothing ready so they will not have to walk around naked and ashamed."

Zechariah 12

10 "Then I will pour out a spirit of grace and prayer on the family of David and on the people of Jerusalem. They will look on me whom they have pierced and mourn for him as for an only son. They will grieve bitterly for him as for a firstborn son who has died.

11 The sorrow and mourning in Jerusalem on that day will be like the great mourning for Hadad-rimmon in the valley of Megiddo."

In context, they don't recognize Him when He returns. That would be especially embarrassing for religious leaders... as in naked and ashamed.

24. Do you think the modern church will be exposed and ashamed that the leaders controlled by the NWO missed Armageddon and led the people astray? Do you think the people who listened to preachers instead of listening to Christ and the Holy Spirit will be disappointed they missed fighting alongside Christ in the Battle of Armageddon?

Yes and yes. Per Zechariah 12:10-11, they will. Especially when they realize "non-Christians" fought alongside our Lord Jesus in the Battle of Armageddon, because many Christians were asleep!

25. Read Revelation 16:16–20. Describe in your own words what this passage depicts. What a sight this will be when the cabal is finally destroyed!

Revelation 16

16 "And the demonic spirits gathered all the rulers and their armies to a place with the Hebrew name Armageddon.

17 Then the seventh angel poured out his bowl into the air. And a mighty shout came from the throne in the Temple, saying, "It is finished!"

18 Then the thunder crashed and rolled, and lightning flashed. And a great earthquake struck—the worst since people were placed on the earth.

19 The great city of Babylon split into three sections, and the cities of many nations fell into heaps of rubble. So God remembered all of Babylon's sins, and he made her drink the cup that was filled with the wine of his fierce wrath.

20 And every island disappeared, and all the mountains were leveled.

21 There was a terrible hailstorm, and hailstones weighing as much as seventy-five pounds fell from the sky onto the people below. They cursed God because of the terrible plague of the hailstorm.""

The thunder and lightning and earthquake symbolism lets us know that the changes we're going to soon witness will rock the entire world. There will be terrifying judgment on those who committed crimes against humanity. Everything will change for the better as the demons are gone and peace settles over the earth. But there will be a lot of upheaval for a while. For those who are part of the NWO, the judgment on them will be terrible beyond words.

26. Since Armageddon is an Information War, where is the Battle of Armageddon?

On the internet / social media.

27. In Revelation 16:17, a voice from the temple shouts "It is done!" Whose voice do you think that is?

The LORD'S voice, the same voice as in Revelation 16:1. He is the beginning and the end of this victory!

28. What does Revelation 16:17 mean by "it is done?" *satan, the beast, and the false prophet have finally been cast into the abyss, and the plan of salvation of humanity has been accomplished!*

29. What is the earthquake in which "the great city was divided city into three parts?" (Revelation 16:19) Think about the three parts of the cabal – Vatican (religious control), City of London (financial control), and Washington DC (military control)

The NWO Tripartite kingdom is ripped apart! Never to be brought back together again!

30. What might the islands and mountains symbolize? (Revelation 16:20)

The NWO leaders have considered themselves mountains high above us! They considered themselves like islands, separate from the rest of us common folk.

31. What might the hail represent that causes the evildoers to curse God? (Revelation 16:21)

The hailstones must be judgment raining down on them, with penalties on earth and in hell greater than anyone could withstand. They deserve it. They had every opportunity to repent and they refused.

32. Summarize this chapter in your own words, and let's take this opportunity to give the LORD praise for His great rescue of humanity!

LORD we praise You for the eradication of our enemies from the earth! Help us to be tough and join with You in bringing down judgment on these demon worshipers. Make Your name glorious in the earth! We praise You for the Millennial Kingdom You have prepared for us, where we will have peace on earth! And health and wealth worldwide! And everyone will know You! We thank You for this amazing promise that is soon to be fulfilled!

20-HARLOTS WILL DO ANYTHING FOR MONEY

"End Times and 1000 Years of Peace" Chapter 19
Revelation Chapter 17

1. Not to be crass, but the only way to understand who the harlot is, is to consider what a harlot does. Basically, anything for money. So, list all the types of groups that will do ANYTHING to help the New World Order with their evil agenda to rule over humanity.

Mainstream Media, Celebrities, Sports Figures, Politicians, District Attorneys, Educational

Institutions, Banks, Tech Giants, Big Pharma, Non-Governmental Agencies.

2. What does it mean that the prostitute/harlot "rules over many waters?" (Also see Revelation 17:15)

> Revelation 17
> 1 *"One of the seven angels who had poured out the seven bowls came over and spoke to me. "Come with me," he said, "and I will show you the judgment that is going to come on the great prostitute, who rules over many waters."*

The Prostitute organizations I listed above control the narrative, the courts, the medicine, the

governments, and the technology in almost every country in the world. Until MAGA!

3. Give examples of how the prostitute commits "fornication" with the kings of the earth. For example: How do they cause people to obey the NWO government rather than God? (Revelation 17:2)

> Revelation 17
> 2 *"The kings of the world have committed adultery with her, and the people who belong to this world have been made drunk by the wine of her immorality."*

They pummel misinformation at the people from every side, deceiving them into believing these lies, taking poisonous vaccines and drugs, destroying their finances, rejecting their families and their country and relinquishing their God-given freedoms.

4. How are the inhabitants of earth *"drunk with the wine of her fornication?"* (Revelation 17:2)

The controllers are drunk with power and the people stagger, not knowing what to believe or who to trust! "People will stagger from sea to sea and wander from border to border searching for the word of the LORD, but they will not find it." (Amos 8:12)

5. Describe in your own words some of the ways the prostitute blasphemes the LORD with a cup full of abomination and wickedness.

> Revelation 17
> *3 "So the angel took me in the Spirit into the wilderness. There I saw a woman sitting on a scarlet beast that had seven heads and ten horns, and blasphemies against God were written all over it.*
> *4 The woman wore purple and scarlet clothing and beautiful jewelry made of gold and precious gems and pearls. In her hand she held a gold goblet full of obscenities and the impurities of her immorality."*

The Prostitute blasphemes the LORD by cursing Him and His people. With every breath they are intent on destroying our livelihoods, our health, our children, our country, and our future. They are happy to send innocents to war and to literally sell children because their hatred of God and His creation.

6. Does the Prostitute seem unhappy? Coerced? Elated? Drunk with power?

The Prostitutes don't seem coerced or unhappy. They seem to be delighted and drunk with power.

7. Is "Mystery Babylon the Great" a particular nation such as America or Russia? Why or why not?

> Revelation 17
> *5 "A mysterious name was written on her forehead: "Babylon the Great, Mother of All Prostitutes and Obscenities in the World."*

No. Babylon has its tentacles of control in every nation.

8. Who is "Mystery Babylon the Great?"

__Mystery Babylon the Great is not a particular nation. Babylon is the hidden group (New World Order cabal) that has controlled and infiltrated every nation for evil purposes.__

9. Give examples of how the Prostitute is *"drunk with the blood of the saints."* (saints is just another name for believers in Christ.)

> Revelation 17
> 6 *"I could see that she was drunk—drunk with the blood of God's holy people who were witnesses for Jesus. I stared at her in complete amazement."*

__Sending innocents to war to make money and gain power, poisoning us and our children with vaccines and food additives and dirty water and air, destroying minds with depression and anxiety and gender confusion, silencing those who fight for truth and justice, the list goes on and on and on.__

10. What is this beast with seven heads and ten horns? Give a likely interpretation of this last beast that was not alive during the time John wrote the Revelation, but would ascend from the bottomless pit.

> Revelation 17
> 7 *"Why are you so amazed?" the angel asked. "I will tell you the mystery of this woman and of the beast with seven heads and ten horns on which she sits.*
> 8 *The beast you saw was once alive but isn't now. And yet he will soon come up out of the bottomless pit and go to eternal destruction. And the people who belong to this world, whose names were not written in the Book of Life before the world was made, will be amazed at the reappearance of this beast who had died."*

__The Prostitute is riding on the NWO Beast that has virtually complete authority and power on earth, humanly speaking. This Beast that was not alive during the time when John wrote the Revelation is likely the "Set" Cult of satanism. It has a temple structure consisting of members__

holding degrees. They participate is unspeakable crimes against humanity, and use that evil to control those inside and outside the cult.

11. Give your thoughts on a likely interpretation of the seven heads and seven mountains of Revelation 17:9. (Possibly the seven NWO control constructs: government, education, entertainment, medical, media/tech, financial, religion?)

> Revelation 17
> *9 "This calls for a mind with understanding: The seven heads of the beast represent the seven hills where the woman rules. They also represent seven kings."*

The seven heads and seven mountains represent the seven constructs for how the NWO controls humanity: government, education, entertainment, medical, media/tech, financial, and religion.

12. Fill in the diagram of the likely interpretation of these kingdoms – five that were fallen as of John's writing, and one that was ruling during John's day, and the seventh one that had not yet come at the time of John's writing, and the eighth/final evil kingdom.

> Revelation 17
> *10 "Five kings have already fallen, the sixth now reigns,*
> *and the seventh is yet to come, but his reign will be brief.*
> *11 The scarlet beast that was, but is no longer, is the eighth king.*
> *He is like the other seven, and he, too, is headed for destruction."*

Kingdom 1 - Fallen - *Egyptian*

Kingdom 2 - Fallen - *Babylonian*

Kingdom 3 - Fallen - *Median*

Kingdom 4 - Fallen - *Persian*

Kingdom 5 - Fallen - *Greek*

Kingdom 6 - Ruling in John's Day - *Roman Empire*

Kingdom 7 - Kingdom Yet To Come - *Holy Roman Empire/ Roman Catholic Empire*
(Holy Roman Catholic Empire)

Kingdom 8 - Final Kingdom (like the 7) *New World Order*

13. Reminder: "the beast that was, and is not" is the 8th Kingdom that ascended from the bottomless pit. I believe that means this Set cult was active long ago, was eradicated, but re-

emerges in the final kingdom.
What do you believe is this kingdom's defining evil characteristic? (See Revelation 17:8 & 11)

We are all amazed that this cult is back because we thought this horrifying satanic sacrifices

and cannibalism had stopped long, long ago.

14. Describe how the ten horns/kingdoms/empires help the New World Order/Babylon gain world domination for a short time.

> Revelation 17
> 12 "The ten horns of the beast are ten kings who have not yet risen to power. They will be appointed to their kingdoms for one brief moment to reign with the beast.
> 13 They will all agree to give him their power and authority."

The NWO set up ten regions worldwide and controlled each nation by installing puppet leaders

who followed the orders of organizations like the UN, the WHO, the IMF, and thereby controlled

every nation's news, their conflicts, their assets, their medicine, etc.

15. Name a few of the "horns" that are currently no longer giving their authority to the New World Order. See map.

10 UN Worldwide Regions

Russia, possibly the Philippines and North Korea.

16. The Beast/False Prophet, Prostitute, and the 10 kingdoms wage war against the Lamb. Who wins?

> Revelation 17
> *14 "Together they will go to war against the Lamb, but the Lamb will defeat them because he is Lord of all lords and King of all kings. And his called and chosen and faithful ones will be with him."*

The LAMB!! Because He is the Lord of all lords and the King of all kings!!

17. How is He able to overcome them? Think about it and explain. (Revelation 17:14)

Because He is wise and patient, and knows the precise way to set humanity free. And He has His faithful ones who follow His every command! He waited 2000 years to have His army ready to fight!

18. Who are the ones who are with Him? (Revelation 17:14)

His Army of awakened warriors!

19. What are their characteristics? (Revelation 17:14)

The chosen and faithful. Hand-selected by the LORD for His own purpose. And proven to be faithful in following Him, no matter what.

20. Take a moment and praise the Lord. He is worthy. Thank you Lord for such an honor to fight alongside You in this epic Battle of Armageddon!

What an honor to be hand-selected by You, Lord. We are are so thankful and to be chosen to be in Your mighty Army for the Battle of Armageddon! You are the Champion of the World!

21. Per the angel, who are the "waters?"

> Revelation 17
> *15 "Then the angel said to me, "The waters where the prostitute is ruling represent masses of people of every nation and language."*

Just like Revelation 17:1 said, the "prostitute rules over many waters" which represents people all over the world. Their evil tyranny has had its tentacles throughout the entire world!

22. Per the angel, how do the "ten horns" feel about the harlot? Why?

> Revelation 17
>
> 16 *"The scarlet beast and his ten horns all hate the prostitute. They will strip her naked, eat her flesh, and burn her remains with fire.*
> 17 *For God has put a plan into their minds, a plan that will carry out his purposes. They will agree to give their authority to the scarlet beast, and so the words of God will be fulfilled."*

The NWO hates the prostitute, especially after they have failed to stop the LORD and His Great Army! The NWO will throw the prostitutes under the bus to try to save their pathetic, scrawny necks.

23. Describe in practical terms what the "ten horns" do to the harlot? (Revelation 17:16-17)

"They will strip her, eat her flesh, and burn her remains with fire." In other words, they will use every legal trick imaginable to lay all the blame on the prostitute, so they can get away scot free. They will lie and cheat and do whatever they have to do to have their minions take the punishment the NWO leaders deserve. But it won't work! White hats have it all! They know each person and each crime that has been committed that caused all the evil that has been wrought on the earth!

24. Per Revelation 17:16-17, who puts it in the New World Order/10 horns' heart to destroy the harlot? That is amazing...they absolutely deserve it!

The LORD HIMSELF!

25. How has the prostitute "ruled" over the kings of the earth?

> Revelation 17
>
> 18 *"And this woman you saw in your vision represents the great city that rules over the kings of the world."*

The prostitutes in the media, the government, entertainment, banks, tech companies, etc., have power over the NWO because they are out front making the actions on behalf of the NWO. The NWO leaders are the hidden hand puppet-masters behind the scenes directing the prostitutes, but they are dependent on the prostitutes to be effective and to succeed.

26. If the harlot fails to control/rule over the people through the government, MSM, medical, education, entertainment etc., what will happen to the New World Order?

The New World Order will be charged with their crimes against humanity, and their evil empire

will collapse!

Revelation 17:17 says "so the words of God will be fulfilled."
Never doubt it.
The LORD will destroy and remove the NWO from the earth!

And that's what happens NEXT!
LET'S GO!

21-BABYLON IS FALLEN

"End Times and 1000 Years of Peace" Chapter 20
Revelation Chapter 18

1. Revelation 18:2 just might have the most wonderful phrase in the entire Bible!

> Revelation 18
> *1 "After all this I saw another angel come down from heaven with great authority, and the earth grew bright with his splendor.*
> *2 He gave a mighty shout:*
> ***"Babylon is fallen—that great city is fallen!***
> *She has become a home for demons.*
> *She is a hideout for every foul spirit,*
> *a hideout for every foul vulture and every foul and dreadful animal."*

Babylon is ***Fallen!***

Babylon is ***Fallen!***

Babylon is ***Fallen!***

2. Babylon is a habitation of/city/home for ***demons*** so when Babylon falls, so do they! (Reminder: Babylon is NOT a particular country. Babylon is NOT America. Babylon is the Criminal Mafia Cabal AKA the New World Order.)

3. Give examples of how the powerful kings, the New World Order criminal cabal and their minions, have grown rich through her delicacies. (e.g. making money by controlling media empires as a mouthpiece for the New World Order's powerful lies.)

> Revelation 18
> *3 "For all the nations have fallen*
> *because of the wine of her passionate immorality.*
> *The kings of the world have committed adultery with her. Because of her desires for*

extravagant luxury,
the merchants of the world have grown rich."

The cabal has made a fortune by fomenting wars where they collect tax revenue for weapons,
and then rob the countries of their assets and gain control by establishing puppet leaders. They
make another fortune by robbing the citizens through confiscatory taxes, and passing that
money to themselves. They have made another fortune by literally selling children. No doubt the
NWO Babylon is a home for demons.

4. What is the warning in Revelation 18:4, and to whom?

> Revelation 18
> *4 "Then I heard another voice calling from heaven,*
> *"Come away from her, my people.*
> *Do not take part in her sins, or you will be punished with her.""*

Come out of the NWO so you won't be punished along with her!

5. What do those in Babylon receive as a penalty for their evil deeds? Revelation 18:6

> Revelation 18
> *5 "For her sins are piled as high as heaven,*
> *and God remembers her evil deeds.*
> *6 Do to her as she has done to others.*
> *Double her penalty for all her evil deeds.*
> *She brewed a cup of terror for others,*
> *so brew twice as much for her."*

They will receive double punishment for their crimes, because they terrorized the entire world.

6. Describe the attitude of the New World Order in Revelation 18:7.

> Revelation 18
> *7 "She glorified herself and lived in luxury,*
> *so match it now with torment and sorrow.*
> *She boasted in her heart,*
> *'I am queen on my throne.*
> *I am no helpless widow,*
> *and I have no reason to mourn.'"*

They feel they don't have to worry about anything because they have plenty of money, and they

don't think they will be held responsible for their crimes. The have believed they were protected in the NWO AntiChrist Club, but now they realize they made a terrible choice to join the NWO.

7. Describe Babylon's downfall.

> Revelation 18
> 8 "Therefore, these plagues will overtake her in a single day — death and mourning and famine.
> She will be completely consumed by fire,
> for the Lord God who judges her is mighty."

Babylon will be destroyed in a single day, just as Revelation 9:15 says "And the four angels who had been kept ready for this very hour and day and month and year were released to kill a third of mankind. (33's – Babylon)." They didn't feel they would every mourn. But now they will. They never feared lack... but now everything, including their freedom, and even their lives, will be stripped from them.

8. Describe the response by the kings (NWO cabal and their minions) to the Fall of Babylon. Why?

> Revelation 18
> 9 "And the kings of the world who committed adultery with her and enjoyed her great luxury will mourn for her as they see the smoke rising from her charred remains.
> 10 They will stand at a distance, terrified by her great torment.
> They will cry out, "How terrible, how terrible for you,
> O Babylon, you great city!
> In a single moment God's judgment came on you."
> 11 The merchants of the world will weep and mourn for her, for there is no one left to buy their goods."

They will be cry and mourn when the NWO is gone, because that's how they became rich and powerful.

9. There are many extravagant goods the merchants gained wealth by selling. Do any of them stand out to you as shocking?

> Revelation 18
> 12 "She bought great quantities of gold, silver, jewels, and pearls; fine linen, purple, silk, and scarlet cloth; things made of fragrant thyine wood, ivory goods, and objects made of expensive wood; and bronze, iron, and marble.

> *13 She also bought cinnamon, spice, incense, myrrh, frankincense, wine, olive oil, fine flour, wheat, cattle, sheep, horses, wagons, and bodies—that is, human slaves."*

Somehow for years most of us missed this part of the verse where they purchase "bodies, that is, human slaves." We realize now that the LORD was telling us about the NWO selling children. But we just couldn't imagine it.

10. Read between the lines...what is this verse pointing to?

> Revelation 18
> *14 "The fancy things you loved so much are gone," they cry.*
> *"All your luxuries and splendor are gone forever, never to be yours again.""*

I'm not going to type what I think this means. But think of precious children. And what demons do. That is why we fight. And that is why we must win.

11. Describe the shock the world will soon experience when the powerful "elite" cabal are arrested and brought to justice for their crimes against humanity. Who are the merchants and why will they lament the New World Order's destruction?

> Revelation 18
> *15 "The merchants who became wealthy by*
> *selling her these things will stand at a distance,*
> *terrified by her great torment. They will weep and cry out,*
> *16 "How terrible, how terrible for that great city!*
> *She was clothed in finest purple and scarlet linens,*
> *decked out with gold and precious stones and pearls!*
> *17 In a single moment all the wealth of the city is gone!"*
> *And all the captains of the merchant ships and their passengers and sailors and crews will stand at a distance.*
> *18 They will cry out as they watch the smoke ascend, and they will say,*
> *"Where is there another city as great as this?"*
> *19 And they will weep and throw dust on their heads to show their grief.*
> *And they will cry out, "How terrible, how terrible for that great city!*
> *The shipowners became wealthy*
> *by transporting her great wealth on the seas.*
> *In a single moment it is all gone."*

The earthquake of judgment that will soon destroy the satanic criminal cabal will shock the world. All we have experienced for the past seven years has helped everyone prepare, but I don't

think any of us can imagine what is coming. People who have been trusted and loved for years will be exposed for their crimes against humanity, arrested, indicted, and prosecuted. The truth about their crimes, with proof, will be available for anyone who wants to know.

Here are a few examples of the merchants who will be sad at the destruction of the NWO: the cartels who transfer the trafficked "goods;" side industries like those that trafficked in the poisonous pharmaceuticals, and the pesticides and additives that poisoned our food; the financial robber-barons who have charged us interest on interest; the demonic music industry, etc.

12. What does Revelation 18:17 likely mean when it says,

> Revelation 18
> *17 "In a single moment all the wealth of the city is gone!"*

Compare that verse with Matthew 24:39.

> Mathew 24
> *39 "People didn't realize what was going to happen until the flood came and swept them all away."*

The NWO's financial collapse will happen quickly and completely, devastating even the NWO leaders, who are deceived into thinking they will be able to avoid this destruction.

13. What is the response by God's people (heavenly humanity), and the apostles and prophets?

> Revelation 18
> *20 "Rejoice over her fate, O heaven and people of God and apostles and prophets! For at last God has judged her for your sakes."*

Such relief that the evil-doers are finally gone and under God's judgment! They can't hurt anyone ever again! Humanity will survive!

14. What does "God has avenged you on her" mean? (God has judged her for your sakes. (Revelation 18:20)

God has judged those who committed crimes against us. They will pay for their crimes!

15. Do you feel that you need the Lord to take vengeance on the New World Order? Yes or No. Why?

Yes! All those who suffered and lost their lives due to the NWO's evil schemes must pay! We cannot have a free society where evildoers get away with literal murder and evil! They must be charged and convicted and punished!

16. How does Revelation 18:20 square with Jesus' command to "love your enemies?" and 1 John 5:16?

> 1 John 5
> 16 *"If you see a fellow believer sinning in a way that does not lead to death (damnation), you should pray, and God will give that person life. But there is a sin that leads to death, and I am not saying you should pray for those who commit it."*

(Note: The sin unto death is the Unpardonable Sin, also known as the Blasphemy of the Holy Spirit, which means to give over your will to demonic control.)

John clearly states in 1 John 5:16 that we are not to pray for those who have willfully and knowingly sold their soul to the devil / sinned the sin unto death / blasphemed the Holy Spirit / committed the unpardonable sin. They are our sworn enemies and they must not be forgiven and given any mercy. "Love your enemies" is a command intended for those who harm us, similar to how Christ loved us and forgave us when we were His enemies.

17. Describe what will likely happen on earth when the *"angel takes up the stone like a great mighty millstone and casts into the sea."*

> Revelation 18
> 21 *"Then a mighty angel picked up a boulder the size of a huge millstone.*
> *He threw it into the ocean and shouted,*
> *"Just like this, the great city Babylon will be thrown down with violence and will never be found again."*

At some point, the cabal will be cast into the "abyss"... gone forever! What a relief that will be! Practically speaking, all the NWO leaders and their minions will be locked behind bars, under judgment, receiving the penalties they deserve for their crimes. Some will be found guilty of treason and crimes against humanity, punishable by death.

18. Compare Revelation 18:21 to Matthew 18:6.
How does this point out the specific evil crimes of the New World Order?

> Matthew 18
> 6 "But whoso shall offend one of these little ones which believe in me, it were better for him that <u>a millstone were hanged about his neck, and that he were drowned in the depth of the sea."</u>

<u>I think when our LORD Jesus was talking about the child he was actually saying that if anyone hurt a child, the punishment would be very awful for them. We just could not imagine what He was referring to. But the evildoers knew.</u>

19. Interesting that this verse uses the word "millstone" also. Describe the destruction of the New World Order Beast/AntiChrist and what stands out to you.

> Revelation 18
> 22 "The sound of harps, singers, flutes, and trumpets will never be heard in you again.
> No craftsmen and no trades will ever be found in you again.
> The **<u>sound of the mill</u>** will never be heard in you again.
> 23 The light of a lamp will never shine in you again.
> The happy voices of brides and grooms will never be heard in you again.
> For your merchants were the greatest in the world,
> and you deceived the nations with your sorceries.
> 24 In your streets flowed the blood of the prophets and of God's holy people
> and the blood of people slaughtered all over the world."

<u>The cabal will never experience joy ever again, because they used satanic sorcery to try to destroy humanity. They intentionally killed people who trusted them! They will pay!</u>

20. Describe what it will be like on earth when the New World Order/Babylon is gone.
Will their eradication be complete? (see Revelation 18:22-24)

<u>Peace on Earth! Health and Wealth and Joy! No more deception! Yes! The NWO will be gone completely!</u>

21. Give examples of the sorceries they have used to deceive humanity. (Revelation 18:23)

<u>They used the WHO, AMA, & CDC to trick people into taking vaccines and unnecessary drugs and falling for a pandemic; they used sorcery to create chemtrails to damage the soil and our</u>

health; They used demonic trickery to brainwash humanity daily through the MSM; they lead

us into endless wars with their fake patriotism propaganda, they used sorcery to create GMOs

that caused nerve damage-induced mental illness, and they used financial trickery to create the

Federal Reserve system. These are just a few examples.

22. Give examples of how the New World Order/Babylon is responsible for "the blood of the prophets, and the saints, and of all those that were slain on earth." (Revelation 18:24)

The vaccines, the pandemic, chemtrails, MSM deception, war machine, GMOs that caused

nerve damage-induced mental illness, the Federal Reserve financial trickery, etc.

23. List some of the ways you will rejoice when Babylon is fallen!

I can't wait to have conversations with people when everyone understands the truth! And where

everyone worldwide knows Jesus and recognizes Him as the King of the world! I can't wait until

we don't have to lock our doors or wonder what crazy news will be reported that day! I can't wait

until everyone is safe from all the NWO wars and man-made diseases and attacks! I can't wait

until everyone has everything they need to take care of their families, and everyone is well and

we see lots and lots of beautiful babies! We will all have to pinch ourselves because we can't even

imagine life without all this mayhem!

24. Since the fall of mankind in the garden of Eden, satan has been the prince of the power of the air.

Thankfully soon he will be cast out.

What we are witnessing – the destruction of the worldwide criminal cabal/AntiChrist is monumental. This amazing salvation of humanity was all purchased by the precious blood of Christ on the cross, so we have victory over the evil principalities.

Let's take this opportunity to tell our Lord Jesus how wonderful He is! And how grateful we are!

Thank You LORD for purchasing humanity with Your own precious blood. You knew the plan

and were the only One who could accomplish that plan to save us. You did it! You have opened the scroll, and started the Great Awakening, just as You promised! You keep all Your promises! So we know You will be the King of the world and every promise of our bright future will be fulfilled! Every knee will bow and every tongue will confess that You are LORD of lords, and King of all kings! You deserve the praise forever and ever everything that has breath! We Praise You LORD!

22-ALLELUIA FOREVER

"End Times & 1000 Years of Peace" Chapter 21
Revelation Chapter 19

1. Just imagine what it will be like when Babylon has finally fallen. After what humanity has been through for all these years. What will be the response of humanity?
Praise! Praise! Praise! And MORE PRAISE!

> Revelation 19
> *1 After this, I heard what sounded like a vast crowd in heaven shouting,*
> *"Praise the Lord!*
> *Salvation and glory and power belong to our God.*
> *2 His judgments are true and just.*
> *He has punished the great prostitute*
> *who corrupted the earth with her immorality.*
> *He has avenged the murder of his servants."*
> *3 And again their voices rang out:*
> *"Praise the Lord!*
> *The smoke from that city ascends forever and ever!"*
> *4 Then the twenty-four elders and the four living beings fell down and worshiped God,*
> *who was sitting on the throne.*
> *They cried out, "Amen! Praise the Lord!"*
> *5 And from the throne came a voice that said,*
> *"Praise our God, all his servants,*
> *all who fear him, from the least to the greatest."*
> *6 Then I heard again what sounded like*
> *the shout of a vast crowd or the roar of mighty ocean waves or the crash of loud thunder:*
> > *"Praise the Lord!*
> > *For the Lord our God, the Almighty, reigns."*

All of humanity will praise the LORD loud and long forever! He rescued us!

Everyone will know. Everyone will be filled with joy!

2. Based on Revelation 19:5–6, who will praise the LORD?

"all his servants, all who fear him, from the least to the greatest."

That surpasses religion and gets to the heart of those who love God and follow Him.

3. What will they say? And how does that encourage you?

"The Lord our God, the Almighty, reigns." God is in control. We have nothing to fear.

4. What ceremony is celebrated?

> Revelation 19
> 7 *"Let us be glad and rejoice, and let us give honor to him. For the time has come for the wedding feast of the Lamb, and his bride has prepared herself.*
> 8 *She has been given the finest of pure white linen to wear." For the fine linen represents the good deeds of God's holy people.*
> 9 *And the angel said to me, "Write this: Blessed are those who are invited to the wedding feast of the Lamb." And he added, "These are true words that come from God."*

A Wedding! Finally our wedding day to Christ has come! And we will live happily ever after!

5. I love that our marriage ceremony happens **before** we are made incorruptible and sinless. In other words, our husband, our Lord Jesus, accepts us as we are. In His eyes we are just perfect! Jesus will dwell with us on earth, as our King and husband. Write down your thoughts on what that will be like.

I love that our Lord will be with us on earth… and we will enjoy peace on earth with Him. And I love that He's not waiting on us to be perfect to come to dwell with us. He's the best. He loves and accepts us just like we are. His love is what transforms us.

6. In Revelation 19:11, heaven opens and there is a white horse. He who sat upon him is Faithful and True. In righteousness he judges and wages war. Who is this?

> Revelation 19
> 11 *"Then I saw heaven opened, and a white horse was standing there. Its rider was named Faithful and True, for he judges fairly and wages a righteous war."*

Our LORD Jesus.

7. According to Revelation 1:7 and other passages, Jesus will return in the clouds. Do you believe Jesus will appear in the literal clouds on a literal white horse? Why or why not?

Revelation 1

7 "Look! He comes with the clouds of heaven. And everyone will see him— even those who pierced him. And all the nations of the world will mourn for him. Yes! Amen!"

No. The clouds and the white horse are symbols for power and royal authority.

8. Acts 1:9-11 describes what happened when our LORD Jesus ascended into Heaven. What is your interpretation of Acts 1:11? Were the angels saying our LORD Jesus will return in the same way, or in a mysterious way?

Acts 1

9 "After saying this, he was taken up into a cloud while they were watching, and they could no longer see him.

10 As they strained to see him rising into heaven, two white-robed men suddenly stood among them. (NLT Version)

*11 "You Galileans!—why do you just stand here looking up at an empty sky? This very Jesus who was taken up from among you to heaven **will come as certainly—and mysteriously—** as he left."* (Message Version)

Our LORD Jesus literally ascended in the clouds. He did not die again, of course. Many interpret this verse to mean that He will return in the exact same way He left. I believe He will return as certainly and AS MYSTERIOUSLY as He left. Not in puffy clouds.

9. What does "his eyes were as a flame of fire" indicate?

Revelation 19

12 "His eyes were like flames of fire, and on his head were many crowns. A name was written on him that no one understood except himself."

He is angry and bringing down judgment on the wicked demon worshipers.

10. What does it mean, practically, for Jesus to have on his head many crowns? (Revelation 19:12)

He will be the head over every sovereign nation. Every nation will submit to His authority.

11. What are your thoughts on "he had a name written that no man knew, but he himself?" (Revelation 19:12)

I believe His new name is likely a Biblical name.

12. What does "he wore a robe dipped in blood" indicate? (See Isaiah 63)

Revelation 19
13 "He wore a robe dipped in blood, and his title was the Word of God."

This blood on His robe is not His own precious blood. It is the blood of His and our enemies, as He is destroying them!

13. Write all of Jesus' names in Revelation 19, and what each one means to you.

Lamb – the One Who gave His life for us, because He loves us so much.

Faithful and True – the One we can count on, and the One who is Truth itself. All aligns to Him.

Name only He understands – the One Who will be revealed.

Word of God – the One Who fulfills all the promises of God.

King of all Kings and Lord of all Lords – the One before Whom every knee will bow and submit.

14. Who are the armies which were in heaven following him on white horses? And what does it mean that they are dressed in the finest of pure white linen?

Revelation 19
14 "The armies of heaven, dressed in the finest of pure white linen, followed him on white horses."

The Army is filled with holy angels and warriors, who are purely fighting to save humanity, so evil will be put down and peace will settle over the earth. Linen is the clothing of priests. The clothing of good deeds. (Revelation 19:8)

15. What does our LORD Jesus do with the sword in His mouth? How does He rule with a rod of iron? And how does He release the fierce wrath of God?

Revelation 19
15 "From his mouth came a sharp sword to strike down the nations. He will rule them with an iron rod. He will release the fierce wrath of God, the Almighty, like juice flowing from a winepress."

He strikes down the wicked. He will force them to submit to His authority and His judgment on them.

This is not just man's judgment on the NWO. Christ releases GOD'S judgment on the AntiChrist!

16. What does our LORD Jesus' title indicate?

> Revelation 19
> *16 "On his robe at his thigh was written this title: King of all kings and Lord of all lords."*

He rules over EVERY earthly authority. That is why Nothing Can Stop What is Coming.

17. What command is given by the angel to the vultures? Who are the vultures?

> Revelation 19
> *17 "Then I saw an angel standing in the sun, shouting to the vultures flying high in the sky: "Come! Gather together for the great banquet God has prepared.*
> *18 Come and eat the flesh of kings, generals, and strong warriors; of horses and their riders; and of all humanity, both free and slave, small and great."*

Devour your enemies! The angel is giving that command from the LORD to the warriors of Armageddon!! YES! This is VERY Biblical! Destroy them! Cast the wicked out! Out! OUT!

18. Revelation 19:18 is quite picturesque. What is this verse describing?

The judgment the NWO satanic cabal will receive. As in public shaming, life imprisonment, and the death penalty. Do NOT hold back judgment! Humanity must know the truth so they will agree.

19. What is happening in Revelation 19:19? Who are the forces arrayed for battle?

> Revelation 19
> *19 "Then I saw the beast and the kings of the world and their armies gathered together to fight against the one sitting on the horse and his army."*

The NWO and their minions are in a full on war with the LORD and His patriots army worldwide.

20. Who is "taken" in Revelation 19:20 and what happens to them? Does that give us insight on when Jesus said one will be "taken?"

> Revelation 19
> *20 "And the beast was captured/taken, and with him the false prophet who did mighty miracles on behalf of the beast—miracles that deceived all who had accepted the mark of the beast and who worshiped his statue. Both the beast and his false prophet were thrown alive into the fiery lake of burning sulfur."*

The KJV version says the Beast was "taken," which means they are captured. That is definitely what our LORD Jesus meant when He told us one would be taken, and one would be left. The one who is taken it taken to prison. The one who is left is left to do a good job in their position of authority.

21. Is there a difference in the punishment received by the beast and false prophet in Revelation 19:20 and the punishment received by the NWO's army in Revelation 19:21? If so, what is it?

> Revelation 19
> *21 "Their entire army was killed by the sharp sword that came from the mouth of the one riding the white horse. And the vultures all gorged themselves on the dead bodies."*

No doubt, the NWO satan-worshipers are cast into hell. But the rest of the army is "killed," as if they receive punishment, but some or all are not cast into eternal hell. The LORD is just and perfect in all His ways. He will judge everyone fairly.

22. What happens to satan?

> Revelation 20
> *1 "Then I saw an angel coming down from heaven*
> *with the key to the bottomless pit and a heavy chain in his hand.*
> *2 He seized the dragon—that old serpent, who is the devil, satan—*
> *and bound him in chains for a thousand years.*
> *3 The angel threw him into the bottomless pit, which he then shut and locked."*

He is bound in chains (prevented from attacking anyone) and thrown into the bottomless pit... hell.

23. For how long? *1,000 years.*

During that period, satan can no longer **attack or deceive** the nations.
(I am personally very, very, very happy about that.)

24. What happens after satan is cast out?

> Revelation 20
> *3 "...so satan could not deceive the nations anymore until the thousand years were finished. Afterward he must be released for a little while."*

After 1,000 years, satan is released for a little while.

25. Put in your own words what John sees in Revelation 20:4?

> Revelation 20
> 4 "Then I saw thrones, and the people sitting on them had been given the authority to judge. And I saw the souls of those who had been beheaded for their testimony about Jesus and for proclaiming the word of God. They had not worshiped the beast or his statue, nor accepted his mark on their foreheads or their hands. They all came to life again, and they reigned with Christ for a thousand years."

The amazing warriors who have stood against the satan worshipers, and have paid a heavy price, will be given authority to judge. It says they were "beheaded" which might be symbolic, or it might be literal. It also says they "all came to life again" which leads us to believe the LORD will resurrect these wise and brave, proven warriors. Whether this is literal or symbolic, the LORD will have these righteous ones judge the wicked, and rule with Him for 1,000 years!

26. What will those sitting on the thrones judge?

They will judge the wicked for all their crimes against humanity and make sure none of them escape justice!

27. Do you think the ability to judge is only in the courts? Or are these given the ability to have good judgment about how everything will be run, from education to entertainment to government to manufacturing, etc.?

The righteous leaders will set everything right! Those skilled in education will Make Education Great Again! Those skilled in finance, will Make Finances Great Again! Those skilled in negotiations with Make World Peace Great Again! Great leaders will lead in every place!

28. What are the defining characteristics of those in Revelation 20:4?

> Revelation 20
> 4 "Then I saw thrones, and the people sitting on them had been given the authority to judge. And I saw the souls of those who had been beheaded for their testimony about Jesus and for proclaiming the word of God. They had not worshiped the beast or his statue, nor accepted his mark on their foreheads or their hands. They all came to life again, and they reigned with Christ for a thousand years."

They spoke the truth and were canceled /killed by the NWO. They did not join the NWO Club or

worship demons.

29. WOW! There are special blessings for those who are part of the first resurrection. What are those blessings listed in Revelation 20:5-6?

> Revelation 20
> 5 *"This is the first resurrection. (The rest of the dead did not come back to life until the thousand years had ended.)*
> 6 *Blessed and holy are those who share in the first resurrection. For them the second death holds no power, but they will be priests of God and of Christ and will reign with him a thousand years."*

It appears this passage says these receive their resurrected bodies that can no die. It could be

symbolic, but it also appears they receive life extension to live and reign with Christ on earth for

1,000 years!

30. What does the first resurrection indicate? If we are reading this accurately, this would be an incomprehensible blessing! See 1 Corinthians 15:23.

> 1 Corinthians 15
> 23 *"But there is an order to this resurrection: Christ was raised as the first of the harvest; then all who belong to Christ will be raised when he comes back."*

The first resurrection in 1 Corinthians 15:23 is Christ's resurrection to His incorruptible body

that can never die. We know that eventually we will all have a resurrected, immortal body like

his.

31. Explain in your own words how the first resurrection is pictured by the Omer festival. Remember, the omer grain is hand-selected and counted for seven weeks, culminating on the Harvest Day of Pentecost/Jubilee. The omer bundle for the first resurrection is hand chosen by the LORD Himself and consists of the 144,000 in the Battle of Armageddon! WOW! See Leviticus 23 for more details.

The LORD is saying He hand-selected His warriors for the Battle of Armageddon! Christ was the

first harvest. And now He has returned and hand-selected His awakened warriors! Just like the

Omer bundle, He has counted on us to fight alongside Him for seven "weeks" or seven years.

32. What could that mean for those who have been part of the Great Awakening and who fought in the digital Battle of Armageddon?

It could mean that they will receive immortal bodies and rule with Christ for 1,000 years.

23-THE MARVELOUS MILLENNIAL REIGN OF CHRIST

"End Times and 1000 Years of Peace" Chapter 22
Excerpts from Isaiah

The Millennial Reign of Christ on earth will be marvelous! Here's what it will be like!!

1. One of my most favorite verses in the Bible is Jeremiah 29:11.

> Jeremiah 29
> *11 "For I know the plans I have for you," says the Lord.*
> *"They are plans for good and not for disaster, to give you a future and a hope."*

Of course this passage is intended for each of us personally to encourage us during difficult times. But what are the <u>worldwide</u> plans the LORD is promising to humanity?

The LORD promised a future and a hope for all of humanity. He has been working toward that

goal for thousands of years, and He will bring that beautiful plan to completion!

2. Praise the LORD that He has promised hope and a future on earth for all of humanity. Put in your own words what Isaiah was describing in Isaiah 60:1–3 about His Glory upon us and the radiance we will have.

> Isaiah 60
> *1 "Arise, Jerusalem! Let your light shine for all to see.*
> *For the glory of the Lord rises to shine on you.*
> *2 Darkness as black as night covers all the nations of the earth,*
> *but the glory of the Lord rises and appears over you.*
> *3 All nations will come to your light;*
> *mighty kings will come to see your radiance."*

When the Millennial Kingdom comes, the righteous will be shown to be the blessed of the LORD.

The meek will inherit the earth! The righteous will rule! Everyone will know it and have to admit we are God's special treasure! The NWO treated us like filth, but the LORD will make His glory shine on us!

3. What does it mean that your sons and daughters will be carried home? (Isaiah 60:4)

> Isaiah 60
> 4 *"Look and see, for everyone is coming home!*
> *Your sons are coming from distant lands;*
> *your little daughters will be carried home."*

Everyone who has been separated from loved ones by the NWO division tactics will be restored to one another. It will be the most wonderful homecoming of all time!

4. Describe the joy of Isaiah 60:5-6 and the abundance of goods and wealth!

> Isaiah 60
> 5 *"Your eyes will shine, and your heart will thrill with joy, for merchants from around the world will come to you.*
> *They will bring you the wealth of many lands.*
> 6 *Vast caravans of camels will converge on you,*
> *the camels of Midian and Ephah.*
> *The people of Sheba will bring gold and frankincense*
> *and will come worshiping the Lord."*

We will receive back everything that has been stolen from us, and then some! The wealth the NWO stole will be returned to the people of every land! There will be plenty for everyone, and plenty for the cities to be made beautiful!

5. What are the offerings of gold and frankincense that will be brought to the LORD?

Everyone worldwide will worship the LORD and give Him praise! Can you imagine it?!

6. What does it mean that "I will accept their offerings" and who is this describing?

> Isaiah 60
> 7 *"The flocks of Kedar will be given to you,*
> *and the rams of Nebaioth will be brought for my altars.*
> *I will accept their offerings, and I will make my Temple glorious."*

God's house will be open for all who believe in Him, and that will be everyone! All will know Him

from the least to the greatest!

7. Unfortunately, the LORD'S house has not been a place of His glory recently. But during the Millennial Kingdom it will be! Put in your own words what it will be like for *"I will make my Temple glorious."* to be fulfilled! (Isaiah 60:7)

The houses of worship will be restored to be a place of prayer! No more infiltrators in God's

house!

No more False Prophets brainwashing the people into following the NWO! The LORD will fill His

house with truth and love and make His house GLORIOUS!

8. What hope does Isaiah 60:8-9 give humanity?

> Isaiah 60
> *8 "And what do I see flying like clouds to Israel,*
> *like doves to their nests?*
> *9 They are ships from the ends of the earth,*
> *from lands that trust in me,*
> *led by the great ships of Tarshish.*
> *They are bringing the people of Israel home from far away, carrying their silver and gold.*
> *They will honor the Lord your God,*
> *the Holy One of Israel, for he has filled you with splendor."*

Those of us who are the scattered tribes of Israel will finally realize our true identity! We will

return to our heritage to worship the LORD in the richness and entirety of His Word. It's not

about moving to a different location. It's about realizing God kept His covenant promises to us,

His people… that He knew we were His people, even if we didn't! And He fulfilled His promise to

Abraham in us!

9. How does Isaiah 60:10 apply to ruined towns in places like Africa, and inner cities of America, and Venezuela, and Afghanistan, and Gaza? Who are these foreigners who will "rebuild your towns"?

> Isaiah 60
> *10 "Foreigners will come to rebuild your towns, and their kings will serve you.*

> *For though I have destroyed you in my anger,*
> *I will now have mercy on you through my grace."*

Countries have been ravaged by the NWO AntiChrist. Assets stolen. Puppet leaders installed.

But soon the wealth taken from the NWO and given back to them and their cities will be rebuilt!

Every place will be restored better than ever before!

10. How will the righteous be treated in the Millennial Kingdom?

> Isaiah 60
> *14 "The descendants of your tormentors will come and bow before you.*
> *Those who despised you will kiss your feet.*
> *They will call you the City of the Lord, and Zion of the Holy One of Israel.*
> *15 "Though you were once despised and hated,*
> *with no one traveling through you,*
> *I will make you beautiful forever, a joy to all generations.*
> *16 Powerful kings and mighty nations will satisfy your every need,*
> *as though you were a child nursing at the breast of a queen.*
> *You will know at last that I, the Lord, am your Savior and your Redeemer,*
> *the Mighty One of Israel."*

We will no longer be despised. We will be treated with honor and respect! Protected and nurtured! The ones who did all this will recognize that the LORD does love us and we are His special treasure.

11. What will all the world know about our Lord Jesus? Isaiah 60:16

The LORD Jesus really is the King of the world and He bought humanity with His own blood, so satan can no longer rule over us and harm us! Praise Him FOREVER!

12. Instead of having broken down leftovers and scraps, what will we enjoy?

> Isaiah 60
> *17 "I will exchange your bronze for gold,*
> *your iron for silver,*
> *your wood for bronze,*
> *and your stones for iron.*
> *I will make peace your leader*
> *and righteousness your ruler."*

Plenty. Everything high quality and beautifully crafted, for everyone worldwide. New roads and bridges and airports. We have worked hard for it and will finally benefit from all our labor!

13. **_Peace_** will be our leader and **_righteousness_** will be our ruler.

> Isaiah 60
> _17b "I will make peace your leader and righteousness your ruler."_

14. Can you imagine no more harm or destruction in all the world? Write down some of the implications of this truth about our future.

> Isaiah 60
> _18 "Violence will disappear from your land;_
> _the desolation and destruction of war will end._
> _Salvation will surround you like city walls,_
> _and praise will be on the lips of all who enter there."_

This madness of violence and destruction will end. Everyone will be safe wherever they go. There will be no more wars. No more bombs. No more children being killed. No more heartbreak. Everyone will be safe and filled with peace and joy! I can't wait!

15. In the Millennial Kingdom, will there be insurance? Lawyers? Courts? Prisons? Hospitals?
Try to put down in words the implications of Isaiah 11:4 and 9.

> Isaiah 11
> _4 "He will give justice to the poor_
> _and make fair decisions for the exploited._
> _The earth will shake at the force of his word,_
> _and one breath from his mouth will destroy the wicked."_
>
> _9 "Nothing will hurt or destroy in all my holy mountain,_
> _for as the waters fill the sea,_
> _so the earth will be filled with people who know the Lord."_

Every one will be treated fairly. The court system will be just! In the Millennial Kingdom there will still be sin and accidents and illness in the world, so there will still be the need for doctors and hospitals, police and courts and lawyers and insurance. But it will not be the absolute mayhem we have endured. Illness will no longer be widespread and chronic. Disease will be

treated properly! We will have what we need rather than worrying all the time about money and insurance and how to pay the bills! Prisons will not be places of hopeless life sentences. Those who have gone astray will receive true rehabilitation and go on to live successful happy lives with their families!

16. Imagine the earth filled with the of knowledge of the Lord... What will that look like?

> Habakkuk 2
> 14 *"For the earth shall be filled with the knowledge of the glory of the Lord, as the waters cover the sea."*

Imagine everyone blessed with happiness and peace. Fulfillment. Joy! Understanding. Beauty. The world filled with the knowledge of glory the LORD and what He has done to rescue humanity!

17. *Put in your own words what the fulfillment of Isaiah 11:6-7 will be like.*

> Isaiah 11
> 6 *"In that day the wolf and the lamb will live together;*
> *the leopard will lie down with the baby goat.*
> *The calf and the yearling will be safe with the lion,*
> *and a little child will lead them all.*
> *7 The cow will graze near the bear.*
> *The cub and the calf will lie down together.*
> *The lion will eat hay like a cow."*

We won't have to fear disaster anymore. The wild animals won't be dangerous. I believe storms will cease too. No more danger! We will be able to relax and enjoy the beautiful world the LORD made for us!

18. Imagine the LORD'S house being <u>established</u> throughout the entire world. I don't believe this means the weak modern Christian church will simply be mass produced worldwide, and other religions eradicated. We will all come together to follow Christ! As the woman at the well said, *"I know the Messiah is coming, the one who is called Christ. When he comes, he will explain everything to us."* (John 4:25)

Write in your own words what it will be like for every person in the world to know and worship the Lord in spirit and in truth.

Isaiah 2

2 "In the last days, the mountain of the Lord's house
will be the highest of all—
the most important place on earth.
It will be raised above the other hills,
and people from all over the world will stream there to worship.
3 People from many nations will come and say,
"Come, let us go up to the mountain of the Lord,
to the house of Jacob's God.
There he will teach us his ways, and we will walk in his paths."
For the Lord's teaching will go out from Zion;
his word will go out from Jerusalem.
4 The Lord will mediate between nations
and will settle international disputes.
They will hammer their swords into plowshares
and their spears into pruning hooks.
Nation will no longer fight against nation,
nor train for war anymore."

Imagine every person connected to the LORD, feeling His Presence, being guided by Him every
day. No longer struggling and being pestered by demonic attacks. Everyone fulfilled and at
peace! Imagine everyone helping each other and giving glory to the LORD. Everyone worshiping
Him, knowing He rescued all of us from the demons! The LORD will settle disputes without war!

19. Do you believe the Lord will dissolve the world religions except for Christianity?
Or that He will clarify their teachings so they all come into alignment with the truth about
Him?
Or something other construct? Describe what it might be like.

I believe the religious constructs worldwide will be transformed! The gatherings places will be
houses of prayer and worship of our Jesus, the Messiah and King of the world! They will be filled
with truth and freedom and unity, rather than propaganda and control. They will honor Him
and foster peace, rather than division. Everyone will recognize our LORD Jesus as the Messiah
who saved humanity!

20. Of course one of my favorite verses is Isaiah 65:20. Put in your own words how

wonderful this will be! And what it might look like, and the implications for the medical community.

> Isaiah 65
> 20 *"No longer will babies die when only a few days old.*
> *No longer will adults die before they have lived a full life.*
> *No longer will people be considered old at one hundred!*
> *Only the cursed will die that young!"*

Babies will be protected and nurtured to live long, healthy lives! No baby will be poisoned with jabs and fake food. We will receive medical treatments that actually work and do not harm! Chronic illness will disappear. We will live strong, healthy lives and our days will begin to increase until they reach 1,000 years! That's what the Book of Jasher says!

21. This all sounds too wonderful to be true! But it is God's Word! Jesus bought all of this for us on the cross! Use this opportunity to praise Him as the wonderful King of this glorious kingdom!!

Thank You Lord from the bottom of our hearts! We can't wait for Your Millennial Kingdom to begin! And for all these blessings to pour down on humanity! And everyone will know that it was all thanks to You and because You died for us on the cross, and fought to destroy the beast NWO AntiChrist! You are the Greatest of All Time!

24-JUDGMENT DAY, GOG AND MAGOG BATTLE, THE BOTTOMLESS PIT

"End Times and 1000 Years of Peace" Chapter 23

Revelation Chapter 20

I probably should put this chapter at the beginning this study guide because it is the key to understanding where we are on the End Times timeline. Once I realized the Gog and Magog Battle happens AFTER the 1000 Years of Peace on earth, everything else in the Book of Revelation started to fall right into place.

1. Why do you think the Gog and Magog Battle is hardly ever discussed? (I'll ask that question again at the end of this study.)

Because if the Soros-controlled seminaries teach about the Gog and Magog Battle, their

faulty End Times teaching falls apart! Once we understand the Gog and Magog Battle is

AFTER the 1000 year Millennial Kingdom of Christ on earth, then we realize we are not

escaping earth in a rapture, but we are staying to fight in the Battle of Armageddon to cast

out the satan worshipers and then enjoy 1000 years of peace on earth! Of course, Soros

never wanted us to believe that!

2. My least favorite Bible verse is Revelation 20:7.

> Revelation 20
>
> 7 *"When the thousand years come to an end, satan will be let out of his prison."*

Why in the world will the LORD loose satan after the 1,000 years of peace on earth?

Because we are destined to have incorruptible bodies and an incorruptible earth, with satan and death vanquished! The final Battle of Gog and Magog ushers in Heaven on earth!

3. In order to answer question #2, remember that during the Millennial Kingdom on earth, there will still be death. Death MUST be conquered. What does that mean for all of humanity for death to be conquered? See 1 Corinthians 15:51- 52.

> 1 Corinthians 15
> 51 *"But let me reveal to you a wonderful secret. We will not all die, but we will all be transformed!*
> 52 *It will happen in a moment, in the blink of an eye, when the last trumpet is blown. For when the trumpet sounds, those who have died will be raised to live forever. And we who are living will also be transformed."*

THAT, my friends, is the reason for the Gog and Magog Battle.

That means when death is conquered, heaven and earth become one. There will be no more separation of loved ones. That's what death really is - separation. No more sorrow or crying. All of that will be done away. Humanity and the earth will be made perfect. Incorruptible!

4. What will satan do when he is loosed?

> Revelation 20
> 8 *"He will go out to deceive the nations—called Gog and Magog—in every corner of the earth. He will gather them together for battle—a mighty army, as numberless as sand along the seashore."*

What satan always does. Deceive. He will gather the deceived ones to fight against the righteous. Of course. Gog and Magog is humanity's final test before we put on immortality!

5. According to Revelation 20:8 are more humans deceived into siding with satan?

It appears they are deceived into siding with satan. We have learned during Armageddon how closely we must listen to the LORD, or we will be deceived into following the NWO. It appears something similar happens during Gog and Magog. The difference is, the people at that time won't be practiced in the art of catching the deception. But then, as now, if we listen closely to Him and keep our "lamps trimmed," He will guide us through.

6. Do you have any idea what it might look like when they "surrounded God's people?" (Revelation 20:9) Try to fast forward in your mind 1000 years. I don't think we can envision what life on earth will be like then, any more than John could've envisioned this digital Internet Battle of Armageddon.

> Revelation 20
> 9 *"And I saw them as they went up on the broad plain of the earth and surrounded God's people and the beloved city."*

I don't think this battle will be in a typical battlefield either. Maybe it will be in a type of META universe? Somehow satan will deceive some people into following evil and attacking the righteous. Gog and Magog will reveal those whose love evil and those who love the LORD.

7. Whatever the Gog and Magog Battle will be sounds terrifying. The LORD knows what it will be like, and He will be there with us and will guide everyone through. What does Revelation 20:9b say the LORD will do then?

> Revelation 20
> 9b *"But fire from heaven came down on the attacking armies and consumed them."*

He will destroy them because He is the King of the world! Evil makes people stupid!

8. Does Revelation 20:9b remind you of an Old Testament Bible story? Which one(s)?

Elijah in the showdown with the priests of Baal (1 Kings 18), when the LORD sent down fire from heaven and burned up the bull sacrifice and the entire altar and trench! Then the prophets of Baal were destroyed!

9. This is one of my favorite Bible verses! How great is this?! The earth will be at complete peace finally!

> Revelation 20
> 10 *"Then the devil, who had deceived them, was thrown into the fiery lake of burning sulfur, joining the beast and the false prophet. There they will be tormented day and night forever and ever."*

Finally, the devil is cast out of earth for good! Forever and ever! Never to be released again!

Along with satan's final ultimate defeat, DEATH IS NO MORE!! I believe that is the moment when we receive our incorruptible bodies! This monumental event is described in 1 Corinthians 15:51–55, Revelation 20:14, and 1 Thessalonians 4:16–17.

Some have interpreted these passages to mean rapture escape from earth. But think of the "rapture" as the moment AFTER THE GOG AND MAGOG BATTLE when we receive our immortal bodies.

> 1 Corinthians 15
>
> *51 "But let me reveal to you a wonderful secret. We will not all die, but we will all be transformed!*
>
> *52 It will happen in a moment, in the blink of an eye, when the last trumpet is blown. For when the trumpet sounds, those who have died will be raised to live forever. And we who are living will also be transformed.*
>
> *53 For our dying bodies must be transformed into bodies that will never die; our mortal bodies must be transformed into immortal bodies.*
>
> *54 Then, when our dying bodies have been transformed into bodies that will never die, this Scripture will be fulfilled.*
>
> *"Death is swallowed up in victory.*
>
> *55 O death, where is your victory?*
>
> *O death, where is your sting?""*

> 1 Thessalonians 4
>
> *16 "For the Lord himself will come down from heaven with a commanding shout, with the voice of the archangel, and with the trumpet call of God. First, the believers who have died will rise from their graves.*
>
> *17 Then, together with them, we who are still alive and remain on the earth will be caught up in the clouds to meet the Lord in the air. Then we will be with the Lord forever."*

> Revelation 21
>
> *4 "He will wipe every tear from their eyes, and there will be no more death or sorrow or crying or pain. All these things are gone forever."*

Describe what is happening in these passages, and what it will be like for humanity.

At the end of the Battle of Gog and Magog, in a moment, in the blink of an eye, humanity will be transformed into immortality! Those who have died will receive their immortal bodies, and those who are alive will too! We will all join the LORD in this elevated place of immortality with resurrected bodies like His. Everyone will be back together on the new earth, and we will all be with the LORD forever. This is His wonderful promise to make all things new!

10. Based on the verses in question #11, what happens to believers' bodies and spirits during this transformation? Do you believe this is also called "the redemption of the body" in Romans 8:23?

> Romans 8
> *23 "And not only they, but ourselves also, which have the first fruits of the Spirit, even we ourselves groan within ourselves, waiting for the adoption, to wit, the redemption of our body." (KJV)*

Our bodies will be changed so they won't grow old, or get tired or sick. The LORD will redeem everything! Including our bodies! Our bodies will be like Adam and Eve's bodies in the Garden of Eden, with one major difference. They won't be able to sin or fall from God.

Just like we have been renewed in our spirit because the Holy Spirit dwells in us, our bodies will be renewed to be like Christ's resurrected body!

11. Do you believe this is yet another parallel passage, talking about the moment we receive our incorruptible bodies?

> 2 Peter 3
> *10 "But the day of the Lord will come as unexpectedly as a thief. Then the heavens will pass away with a terrible noise, and the very elements themselves will disappear in fire, and the earth and everything on it will be found to deserve judgment."*

Yes, when the heavens pass away with fervent heat is the moment the evildoers are burned up, and the righteous shine through like gold! The earth becomes like heaven! Only the immortal can dwell in heavenly perfection! The great day will reveal those who truly love the LORD!

12. If 1 Corinthians 15:51–55, Revelation 20:14, and 1 Thessalonians 4:16–17 occur **AFTER THE BATTLE OF ARMAGEDDON** and describe humanity putting on immortality, what effect does that have on the modern day Rapture teaching, the Beast taking over the world, and the LORD destroying all of humanity?

(That explains why the Gog and Magog battle is never discussed.)

Then clearly 1 Thessalonians 4:16-17 is not talking about Christians escaping earth before the Tribulation. It is talking about our transformation to immortality after Gog and Magog! Oopsies!

13. If we are not escaping earth, and God is NOT destroying humanity indiscriminately, what is our mindset toward humanity, the world, and our future?

That the LORD loves them too and is rescuing them too, and that we all need to join together to fight against the evil satanic NWO AntiChrist so we can all enter into the Millennial Kingdom of Christ on earth! The NWO definitely doesn't want humanity united!

14. What happens after the Battle of Gog and Magog?
> Revelation 20
> *11 "And I saw a great white throne and the one sitting on it.*
> *The earth and sky fled from his presence, but they found no place to hide.*
> *12 I saw the dead, both great and small, standing before God's throne.*
> *And the books were opened, including the Book of Life.*
> *And the dead were judged according to what they had done, as recorded in the books.*
> *13 The sea gave up its dead, and death and the grave gave up their dead.*
> *And all were judged according to their deeds.*
> *14 Then death and the grave were thrown into the lake of fire.*
> *This lake of fire is the second death.*
> *15 And anyone whose name was not found recorded in the Book of Life was thrown into the lake of fire."*

The Great White Throne judgment! The LORD Jesus will judge everyone according to their deeds. There will be no place to hide.

15. At this point the demon worshipers are in the abyss. So what happens to the rest of humanity at the White Throne Judgment?
> Revelation 20
> *13 "The sea gave up its dead, and death and the grave gave up their dead. And all were judged according to their deeds."*

The evildoers will spend eternity in torment in their corrupted decayed body. Ew! And the righteous will be rewarded according to their deeds and live forever in perfect joy!

16. Revelation 20:13 says "all were judged according to their deeds."
How does that square with being justified by faith, and not by works?
(See Romans 5:1, Ephesians 2:8–9, Titus 3:5, Galatians 2:16)

We are justified – made legally righteous - by faith in Christ. His atoning blood alone can

remove sin. But how can we judge whether someone's faith is genuine or not? By their deeds.

Talk is cheap. The LORD will judge every man by their actions.

17. What does James mean in James 2:18-20.

> James 2
> 18 "Now someone may argue, "Some people have faith; others have good deeds."
> But I say, "How can you show me your faith if you don't have good deeds?
> I will show you my faith by my good deeds."
> 19 You say you have faith, for you believe that there is one God. Good for you!
> Even the demons believe this, and they tremble in terror.
> 20 How foolish! Can't you see that faith without good deeds is useless?"

The demons believe God's Word is true, and tremble in terror. But they don't have saving

faith. True saving faith produces good deeds. Our love for the LORD is evident by our

actions.

18. Let's be honest. It would take a long - long - long - long time to sit through every court proceeding of every man, woman, and child, small and great. Even forever might not be long enough! Scripture leads us to believe there will be a "knowing." Much like these verses.

> 1 Corinthians 13
> 12 "Now we see things imperfectly, like puzzling reflections in a mirror, but then we
> will see everything with perfect clarity. All that I know now is partial and incomplete,
> but then I will know everything completely, just as God now knows me completely.
> 13 But on the judgment day, fire will reveal what kind of work each builder has done.
> The fire will show if a person's work has any value.
> 14 If the work survives, that builder will receive a reward.
> 15 But if the work is burned up, the builder will suffer great loss.
> The builder will be saved, but like someone barely escaping through a wall of flames."

Does it appear we will all simply "know" each others works, good and bad, without the need for explanation?

Yes, I don't foresee long drawn out Perry Mason type trials at the White Throne Judgment.

We will see everything with perfect clarity. We will know completely. The fire will show a

person's faith. For example, it will be obvious to everyone that those who worked day after day to destroy humanity, clearly do not have saving faith in Christ.

19. Will believers be judged? What other Bible verses apply?

> 2 Corinthians 5
> *10 "For we must all stand before Christ to be judged.*
> *We will each receive whatever we deserve for the good or evil we have done in this earthly body."*

Yes, the LORD will determine the rewards we'll receive, by judging our faith, which produced our actions. Also, 1 Corinthians 4:5 makes clear that our LORD Jesus will be looking at our motives when He judges us. "So don't make judgments about anyone ahead of time—before the Lord returns. For he will bring our darkest secrets to light and will reveal our private motives. Then God will give to each one whatever praise is due."

20. Try to put into your own words this amazing transformation that will happen on earth. Don't worry if it seems indescribable.

> Revelation 20
> *14 "Then **death and the grave were thrown into the lake of fire**. This lake of fire is the second death."*

No more death. Like the Garden of Eden. That means people won't die. Think of Methusaleh. Animals won't die. Think of old turtles. Trees won't die. Think of the Redwood Forest. Everything will be set to auto-renew. Lush. Vibrant. Never old. Always new.

21. How does Revelation 20:14 compare with 1 Corinthians 15:23–25?

> 1 Corinthians 15
> *23 "But there is an order to this resurrection: Christ was raised as the first of the harvest; then all who belong to Christ will be raised when he comes back.*
> *24 After that the end will come, when he will turn the Kingdom over to God the Father, having destroyed every ruler and authority and power.*
> *25 For Christ must reign until he humbles all his enemies (including death) beneath his feet."*

Christ will reign in His Millennial Kingdom until He destroys death and the grave at Gog and Magog. Then He will hand His Kingdom back to God the Father. Mission Accomplished!

22. What does Revelation 20:14 mean by "the lake of fire is the second death" compared to the "first death"? (See Ephesians 2:1 and 1 Corinthians 15:22 regarding the first

death.)

Everyone has experienced the first death which is our separation from God because of sin,

as "everyone dies because we are Adam's seed." (1 Corinthians 15:22) and "Once you were

dead because of your disobedience and your many sins." (Ephesians 2:1) This first death

culminates in our physical death. And the Bible talks about a second death. The second

death is when the damned are reunited eternally with their rotting corpses. Along with

everything in hell which is dead, rotting, and putrid. Always dying, but never annihilated.

Hellish.

23. What is the Book of Life?
(See Revelation 20:15, Revelation 17:8, Revelation 13:8, and Revelation 3:5)

The Book in which are written every name of those who have true living faith in God.

24. Is the "Lake of Fire" eternal? (See Mark 9:44, Mark 9:46, and Mark 9:48)

Yes. As our Lord Jesus said, "Where the maggots never die and the fire never goes

out." (Mark 9:48)

25. The beast and the false prophet are judged and cast into the abyss after the Battle of Armageddon. But their final judgment is when they receive back their dead bodies after Gog and Magog, when death is cast into hell also.

The spirits of our ancestors in Heaven will receive their incorruptible bodies with their amazing abilities, much like our Lord Jesus' resurrected body. But the damned will receive their **corruptible** bodies at the Judgment Day. How will this add to their torment, like our Lord Jesus described with "Where the maggots never die and the fire never goes out?"

The damned will get no relief day or night from their torment. When they receive their

corrupted bodies, that will only add to their pain and misery. Unimaginable torment!

26. So now that you have studied this chapter, I will ask this question again.
Why do you think the Gog and Magog battle is hardly ever discussed?

Because if the Soros-controlled seminaries teach about the Gog and Magog Battle, their

faulty End Times teaching falls apart! Once we understand the Gog and Magog Battle is

AFTER the 1000 year Millennial Kingdom of Christ on earth, then we realize we are not escaping earth in a rapture, but we are staying to fight in the Battle of Armageddon to cast out the satan worshipers and then enjoy 1000 years of peace on earth! Of course, Soros never wanted us to believe that!

Ready to study what happens AFTER the Battle of Gog and Magog? Just turn the page!

25-UNSPEAKABLE JOY!

"End Times and 1000 Years of Peace" Chapter 24
Revelation Chapter 21

Revelation 21 is the culmination of the LORD'S promise to us, and what humanity has been striving after for 7000 years. After the 1000 years of peace on earth, it will have been 8000 years working toward and anticipating this Great Day! That is why this chapter is titled "Unspeakable Joy!"

1. What is the future the LORD has prepared for us after the Gog and Magog battle?

__Peace on earth and no more death, sorrow, or crying! Heaven literally on earth!__

2. Put in your own words what a new heaven and a new earth will be like.

> Revelation 21
> *1 "Then I saw a new heaven and a new earth, for the old heaven and the old earth had disappeared. And the sea was also gone.*
> *2 And I saw the holy city, the new Jerusalem, coming down from God out of heaven like a bride beautifully dressed for her husband.*
> *3 I heard a loud shout from the throne, saying, "Look, God's home is now among his people! He will live with them, and they will be his people. God himself will be with them."*

Will there be any separation between heaven and earth? Try to describe it. Remember, at this point there will be no death. God's people will all have incorruptible bodies.

__This verse describes the union between the new heaven and the new earth. Everything will be made new and incorruptible! And best of all, the LORD will live with His people... ALL His people. There will be no difference between heaven and earth. "God Himself will be with them." No worries. No evildoers. Nothing to cause the slightest alarm!__

3. Will the LORD dwell with us physically as our King on earth during the Millennial

Kingdom?

> Obadiah 1
> 21 *"Those who have been rescued will go up to Mount Zion in Jerusalem to rule over the mountains of Edom.*
> *And the Lord himself will be king!"*

Yes, according to Obadiah and other passages.

4. Try to imagine Revelation 21:4 and put it into your own words. Praise the LORD for this unspeakable gift.

> Revelation 21
> 4 *"He will wipe every tear from their eyes, and there will be no more death or sorrow or crying or pain. All these things are gone forever."*

Imagine all our loved ones reunited. Safe and whole. Complete joy! All our suffering will be just a distant memory, left there to remind us of how thankful we our for our Wonderful Savior!

5. What else will our LORD Jesus do in His reign of Heavenly Earth? Enjoy!

> Revelation 21
> 5 *"And the one sitting on the throne said, "Look, I am making everything new!" And then he said to me, "Write this down, for what I tell you is trustworthy and true."*
> *6 And he also said, "It is finished! I am the Alpha and the Omega—the Beginning and the End. To all who are thirsty I will give freely from the springs of the water of life.*
> *7 All who are victorious will inherit all these blessings, and I will be their God, and they will be my children."*

Can you imagine EVERYTHING NEW?!! And it can't get worn out! Think of Maralago for everyone worldwide! There will be no lack. No disappointment. All fulfilled. Everyone will inherit the blessings of victors! And they will sense the love the LORD has for them individually as His children. Fullness of joy that will never run out!

6. Who is excluded and where will they be?

> Revelation 21
> 8 *"But cowards, unbelievers, the corrupt, murderers, the immoral, those who practice witchcraft, idol worshipers, and all liars—their fate is in the fiery lake of burning sulfur. This is the second death."*

In the fiery lake of burning sulfur. Forever.

7. Tell in your own words about the beautiful new heaven and the new earth we will enjoy, and bask in the glory which is our future!

Revelation 21

9 "Then one of the seven angels who held the seven bowls containing the seven last plagues came and said to me, "Come with me! I will show you the bride, the wife of the Lamb."

10 So he took me in the Spirit to a great, high mountain,

and he showed me the holy city, Jerusalem, descending out of heaven from God.

11 It shone with the glory of God and sparkled like a precious stone— like jasper as clear as crystal.

12 "The city wall was broad and high, with twelve gates guarded by twelve angels.

And the names of the twelve tribes of Israel were written on the gates.

13 There were three gates on each side—east, north, south, and west.

14 The wall of the city had twelve foundation stones, and on them were written the names of the twelve apostles of the Lamb.

15 The angel who talked to me held in his hand a gold measuring stick to measure the city, its gates, and its wall.

16 When he measured it, he found it was a square, as wide as it was long. In fact, its length and width and height were each 1,400 miles.

17 Then he measured the walls and found them to be 216 feet thick (according to the 77 human standard used by the angel).

18 The wall was made of jasper, and the city was pure gold, as clear as glass.

19 The wall of the city was built on foundation stones inlaid with twelve precious stones: the first was jasper, the second sapphire, the third agate, the fourth emerald,

20 the fifth onyx, the sixth carnelian, the seventh chrysolite, the eighth beryl, the ninth topaz, the tenth chrysoprase, the eleventh jacinth, the twelfth amethyst.

21 The twelve gates were made of pearls—each gate from a single pearl!

And the main street was pure gold, as clear as glass.

22 I saw no temple in the city, for the Lord God Almighty and the Lamb are its temple.

23 And the city has no need of sun or moon, for the glory of God illuminates the city, and the Lamb is its light.

24 The nations will walk in its light, and the kings of the world

will enter the city in all their glory.

25 Its gates will never be closed at the end of day because there is no night there.

26 And all the nations will bring their glory and honor into the city.

27 Nothing evil will be allowed to enter, nor anyone who practices shameful idolatry and dishonesty—but only those whose names are written in the Lamb's Book of Life."

Heaven on earth sounds so beautiful! Whether the streets are made of literal gold or not, the

point is that gold is no longer needed to survive. Everyone has plenty. Everyone we be able

to enjoy heaven on earth, and fulfill their God-given assignment freely, without any stress or struggle. The LORD will fill the world with His wonderful presence, so everyone abides in continual peace. Ahhhhh.....

26-ADDENDUM

"End Times and 1000 Years of Peace" Heavenly Star Signs

To learn more about the heavenly star signs, I recommend downloading the online planetarium from *Stellarium.org*.

The top arrow is the Date window.

The middle arrow is for the Sky and Viewing Options.

The bottom arrow is the Search window.

Turn on the items with the arrows on the left. (constellation label, lines, and art)

Turn off the items with the second set of arrows. (ground, atmosphere, cardinal points, meteor showers and satellites)

Turn on the item with the single arrow. (azimuthal mount)

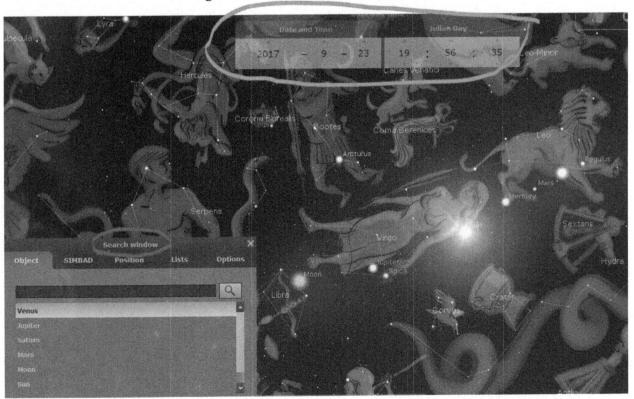

Once you make those selections, the constellations will appear on your screen.

When you select the Date option on the left menu, you will see the date and time window. (circled at top bar)

When you select the Search option on the left menu, you will see the search window. (circled at left)

In the Search window, when you select Jupiter, you will see four red marks around Jupiter. You will also see Jupiter's data on the left. (right click to remove the data from the screen.)

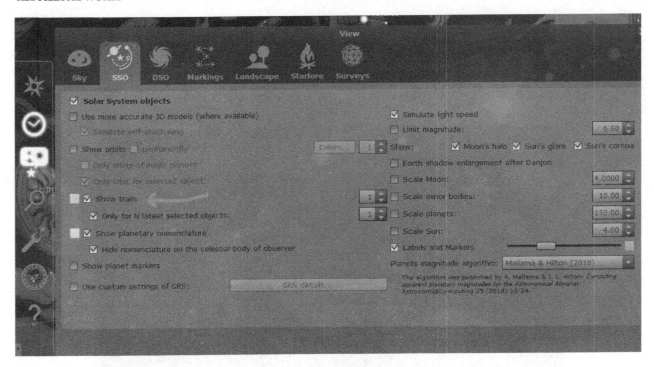

Once Jupiter is selected, in the Sky & Viewing Options window, click the SSO tab, and then select "Show Trails" to be able to easily see the track the wandering stars create.

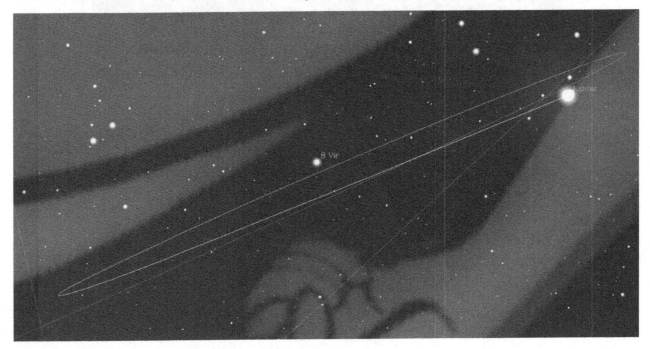

This is the loop created by Jupiter/Melchidezek – a 42-week gestation period. (1260 days, 3 1/2 years, time, times, and half a time.)

With the Stellarium planetarium software you can become familiar with the constellations and the paths of the wandering stars. That is helpful in decoding star signs from the LORD that He has placed in His Holy Word.

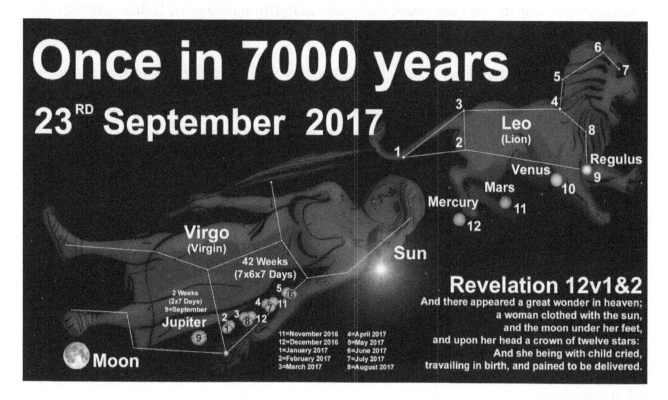

A very important star sign in the Book of Revelation is called **"The Sign of the Son of Man."**
The loop in the image at left was formed inside Virgo, as if it was "travailing in birth pains."

Jupiter/Melchizedek entered Virgo on the day President Trump was elected in 2016! How's THAT for Biblical! Jupiter's loop completed all the exact elements from Revelation 12:1-2.

Our Lord Jesus told us in Matthew 24:30-31 to watch for this sign.

"Then the sign of the Son of Man will appear in heaven, and then all the tribes of the earth

will mourn, and they will see the Son of Man coming on the clouds of heaven with power and

great glory. And He will send His angels with a great sound of a trumpet, and they will gather

together His elect from the four winds, from one end of heaven to the other."

The Sign of the Son of Man is also known as **"A Woman in Labor"** throughout the Old Testament. Most of the time, the verse says those who see a "Woman in Labor" will be in great panic! As if, the New World Order is panicking because humanity is waking up and they can't stop it! "We have heard the report of it; Our hands grow feeble. Anguish has taken hold of us, Pain as of **a woman in labor**." (Jeremiah 6:24)

2. Now that you see how Jupiter/Melchizedek makes "loops" in the heavens, and you saw how precisely the loop was created in Virgo's "womb," now let's follow Jupiter/Melchizedek for more clues from the loops it creates. I think this just might give us a clue about the seven bowls of God's wrath that He is stirring up! This is speculation, but it is possible that after the birth phase, Jupiter makes seven loops (or bowls), culminating in the destruction.

For this assignment, enter Stellarium and search Jupiter, then in the Sky and Viewing Options window, click the SSO tab, and then select "Show Trails" to be able to easily see the track Jupiter through the heavens from September 23, 2017 to March 2024.

Let's plot each of the loops/bowls one by one, as each phase that goes by, the LORD exposes the New World Order more and more. This is what we have been witnessing on earth. Again, this is somewhat speculation as to the meaning of this star sign. We are searching for truth, as the LORD gives us understanding.

Jupiter/Melchizedek's loops/bowls likely coincide with the bowls of God's wrath in Revelation 16, which are exposing and bringing down the New World Order cabal beast!

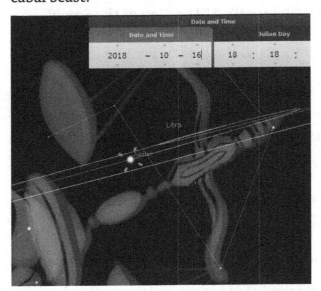

Loop/Bowl 1

This loop/bowl completed in October 2018 spells the Judgment Day for the New World Order!

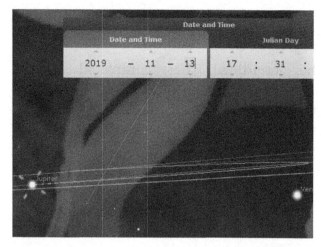

Loop/Bowl 2

This loop/bowl that completed in November 2019 is the wrestling phase in Ophiucus- the serpent wrestler. We are wrestling control from the cabal.

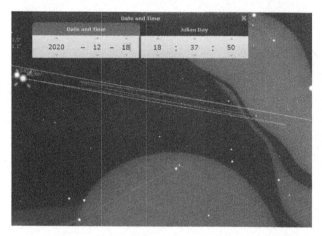

Loop/Bowl 3

The zigzag/bowl that completed in December 2020 in Sagittarius is "shooting arrows" at the New World Order. Damaging them, but not yet fully destroying them.

Loop/Bowl 4

This loop/bowl completed in January 2022 represents the Great Awakening in Aquarius and Capricorn.

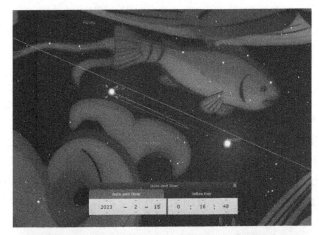

Loop/Bowl 5

The loop/bowl that completed in February 2023 represents the fish breaking free from the lies and oppression of the NWO sea monster!

(Think of fish as those who believe in God, just as the disciples were told to be fishers of men.)

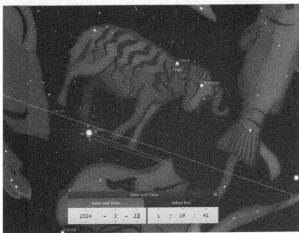

Loop/Bowl 6

The loop/bowl completed March 2024 represents the redemption of humanity… rescued from the clutches of the NWO. (Aries represents Christ as the Lamb of God who redeems the world.)

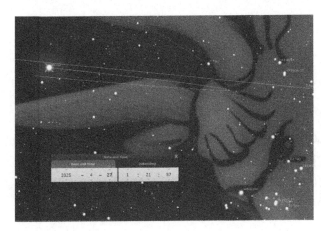

Loop/Bowl 7

Jupiter completes a zigzag/bowl in Taurus in April 2025 as it is goring the New World Order to utter destruction.

2. Now let's find the angel/messenger in the Stellarium online planetarium! Revelation 10 talks about an angel that has feet like fire! Which wandering star might that be? (see "End Times and 1000 Years of Peace" Chapter 11)

Now let's determine in which constellation in the heavens this star will perform its sign. This angel has a very important job! He will give John a little book to read that will make his stomach bitter. That was when John was redpilled! He experienced the Great Awakening! God poured out His Spirit of understanding on John. Which constellation might be a picture of God pouring out His Spirit on all humanity?

Follow that wandering star in the heavens until you see it create a sign in that particular constellation! In the Search Window select that wandering star, and then select the Sky & Viewing Options window so you can select "Show Trails" to see the track it creates.

Follow that star until it appears in the constellation which pictures God pouring out His Spirit on all flesh...and what do you see? Was there a special sign? Did something huge happen to awaken humanity at that time?

Mercury completed a loop in Aquarius, which was a sign of the awakening of humanity.

At that time all of humanity experienced the covid pandemic, which was a worldwide awakening to the NWO and their cruel tyranny.

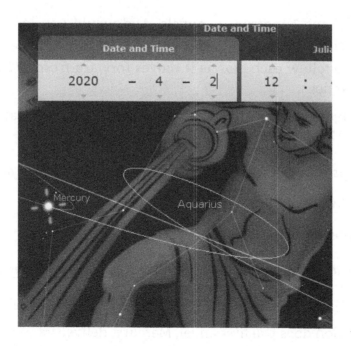

3. Next, let's look at a very intricate sign. This is an additional part of the Sign of the Son of Man.

Mercury – 1st Angel

Venus – 2nd Angel

Mars – 3rd Angel

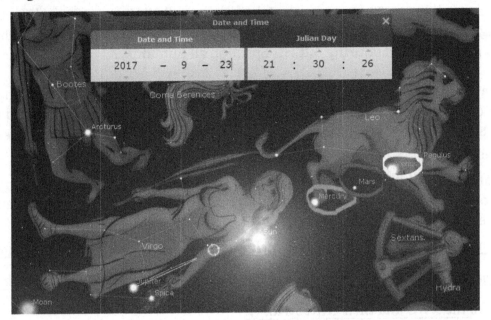

Revelation 14 talks about 3 messenger angels. And would you look at that? Three messenger angels are lined up in a row in the "Sign of the Son of Man."

Your assignment is to follow each star as it moves forward from 9/23/2017 and see what each "angel" star does.

4. Does Mercury conjoin temporarily with another wandering star on its way to complete its mission? Which star? What might this symbolize?

Yes... Mercury conjoins with Jupiter, the Christ star. As if to receive a message from the LORD, and then go deliver that message.

5. What is the message in Revelation 14:6-7 of the first angel, Mercury?

"Fear God," he shouted. "Give glory to him. For the time has come when he will sit as judge. Worship him who made the heavens, the earth, the sea, and all the springs of water."

6. In which constellation does the first angel, Mercury, deliver its message? How does that constellation's symbolism coincide with the angel's message?

Libra - the scales of justice! Because it is time for the evildoers to be judged!

7. Does Venus conjoin temporarily with another wandering star on its way to complete its mission? Which star? What might this symbolize?

Yes. Venus conjoins with Jupiter, the Christ star. As if to receive a message from the LORD, and then go deliver that message.

8. What is the message in Revelation 14:8 of the second angel, Venus?

"Babylon is fallen—that great city is fallen—because she made all the nations of the world drink the wine of her passionate immorality."

9. In which constellation does the second angel, Venus, deliver its message? How does that constellation's symbolism coincide with the angel's message?

Scorpio – representing conflict and war! Christ has the NWO AntiChrist in his grasp!

10. Does Mars conjoin temporarily with another wandering star on its way to complete its mission? Which star? What might this symbolize?

Yes.. Mars conjoins with Jupiter, the Christ star. As if to receive a message from the LORD, and then go deliver that message.

11. What is the message in Revelation 14:9-11 of the third angel, Mars?

"Anyone who worships the beast and his statue or who accepts his mark on the forehead or on the hand must drink the wine of God's anger… and be tormented day and night forever."

12. In which constellation does the third angel, Mars, deliver its message? How does that constellation's symbolism coincide with the angel's message?

In Ophiucus – the Serpent Wrestler. Ophiucus represents our LORD Jesus as the One who wrestles the NWO snake and will defeat them.

13. Remember that I told you the Book of Revelation is filled with heavenly star signs? Well, here's another one! *"I saw another sign in heaven, great and marvelous, having the seven last plagues, for in them is filled up the wrath of God."* (Revelation 15:1)

This wonder is a bit more esoteric. The LORD did not give us many clues in Revelation

15, and I don't know of other clues in Scripture, so we will have to speculate on what this sign could be, until we have greater light. We know Revelation 15 includes a sign in the heavens. And we know the sign includes seven last plagues.

Which constellation includes a famous constellation of seven stars, called the "seven sisters?" That is likely a clue.

Taurus the Bull

14. Something unusual happened in Taurus in 2020. Venus left the usual ecliptic path on February 17, 2020 and entered into Taurus to perform a zigzag sin wave through Pleiades, around the left horn, and through Taurus' red eye. (You can toggle the ecliptic path on and off in the Stellarium planetarium by pressing the "C" key.)

It is possible that this is the sign of the wrath of God from Revelation 15. During this period, we have information that leads us to believe the abomination of desolation of child sacrifices in underground tunnels was stopped. That would be a great and marvelous heavenly wonder indeed!

For this assignment, open the Stellarium app, search Venus, then in the Sky & Viewing Options window, click the SSO tab, and then select "Show Trails" to be able to easily see the track Venus makes through Taurus from 2/17/20 through 7/10/20.

For more information about the Biblical meanings of the stars, check out the Biblical Astronomy videos on the *FreedomForce.LIVE* website. The heavens really do declare the glory of God!

EPILOGUE

Now that you have discovered the wonderful truth about End Times, it's time to share the Good News of the Kingdom everywhere! Everyone needs to know the truth! Eventually everyone will.

But for now, most Christians are scared to pieces! It's our job to coax them out from under the bed, and share the wonderful truth that the Millennial Kingdom of Christ is just over that next hill. Let's all join the fight for humanity and watch His Kingdom come and His will be done on earth as it is in Heaven!

If you would like to enjoy the camaraderie of others who are awake to this wonderful truth, join us on the social media listed on FreedomForce.LIVE. 1000+ videos with more good news to share! See you there!

Love,

Melissa Redpill The World

REVELATION DECODE SERIES

It's finally time to know the truth about Revelation. And it's not what you think... End Times is actually Good News for humanity! The "Revelation Decode" series removes all the deception we were force-fed from Hollywood and the Deep Church, and now these mysteries make sense!

"End Times and 1000 Years of Peace" decodes the Book of Revelation and Daniel's End Times prophecies.

"End Times Major Clues from Minor Prophets" decodes the Minor Prophets books revealing that they were telling us all about the Great Awakening, the Judgment of the New World Order, and the Millennial Kingdom of Christ on earth!

"End Times - This is Biblical!" shows how seventeen Bible stories are a roadmap for us on how we are destroying the NWO Beast of Revelation. What we are experiencing is Biblical.... literally!
The entire Bible from cover-to-cover tells us this is the Great Day we have been waiting for all our lives. The LORD even gave us a sign in the heavens on September 23, 2017, much like the Bethlehem star, and told us over 20 times to watch for it!
There is nothing to fear.
There is great cause of excitement and anticipation!
And it's all in the "Revelation Decode" series and on FreedomForce.LIVE.
ENJOY!

End Times And 1000 Years Of Peace

Have you ever wanted to understand the book of Revelation, but all the symbolism left you dazed and confused? And the movies and books on the subject make it even worse! Well, FINALLY the truth about End Times has been revealed! It might take reading this book a few times, to sort out all the confusion and misinformation we were told. But, this is the wonderful truth. Finally. And, best of all, after we get through these very strange "End Times," we truly will enter 1,000 years of peace on earth. Enjoy.

End Times Major Clues From Minor Prophets

I don't think it's a far stretch to say that most people who read the Bible, don't spend much time reading the Minor Prophets. Minor Prophets, you say? Who are they? My point exactly. I think we figured those books were likely about some stale old history of the Israelites, and had little or no practical bearing on us now or on our future. Wrong-O.

Many of us have spent our time mostly in the New Testament learning about Jesus. Of course, learning about Jesus is wonderful. But those Minor Prophet books are there for a reason. And now we are discovering why.
Would you believe that the Minor Prophets tell us about the NWO cabal...
and about the Great Awakening...
and how a Great Army will rise up and defeat the NWO enemy...
and humanity will enter into wonderful days of health and wealth and peace and joy?
Yep. Clear as a bell. That's what I'm going to decode for you in this book.

End Times - This Is Biblical!: 17 Bible Stories Happening Before Our Eyes

For most of my life I have been telling Bible stories to children. I've told the historical accounts of God's people and the miracles the LORD worked time and time again. I love God's Word. I love each and every historical account. I could tell them all day long and in my sleep! They are the most riveting and inspiring stories ever...and most importantly they are the foundation of our confidence of the LORD'S sovereignty, His great power, and His great love for humanity.

I just never imagined that I would see these very Bible stories that I've been retelling all my life, playing out before my very eyes. When I first realized we were experiencing the Book of Revelation, I began to ask the LORD to help me understand and unravel the knots of lies we had been told about End Times. We had been misled and frightened to pieces so that many believers are hiding under the bed and have their bags packed to escape earth. Obviously that's exactly where the mafia cabal criminal Deep State Beast in Revelation wants believers to be, instead of in the fight exposing their crimes. But I am here to tell you this is the End Times for them and 1,000 years of peace on earth for humanity!

So get out from under the bed and let's join the fight. This book is not specifically about Revelation or End Times. If you want the true decode of Revelation, check out my Bestseller, "End Times and 1000 Years of Peace." You can also check out my other Bestseller, "End Times - Major Clues from Minor Prophets" to see how the LORD promised through the Minor

Prophets that this day would come, when humanity would wake up and cast out these evil-doers. And the Minor Prophets told us about our great victory just up ahead!

But this book has been on my heart to write since I woke up just before President Trump was elected...the first time. I have been telling these stories for so long, and now I get to tell how they are being fulfilled in our day! We as humanity are living out and experiencing them all. How cool for the LORD to create this amazing Biblical road map for us!

You will love it!

PRAISE FOR AUTHOR

5.0 out of 5 stars Biblical Truth Telling Revealed
Reviewed in the United States on June 20, 2024
Verified Purchase
This is one out of the three in this series that Melissa put together and they are all fantastic. Complete and thorough breakdowns of Old Testament and all the key individuals that I never learned about. You can very clearly read that this woman has genuine solid knowledge of her Bible and her discernment is spot on. The best is it feels like she's speaking directly to you in a very matter of fact easy going way but with true conviction and wisdom. I love them all!

Amazon Customer
5.0 out of 5 stars Amazing book decoding the very difficult Book of Revelation.
Reviewed in the United States on June 21, 2024
Verified Purchase
End Times and 1000 Years of Peace is a brilliant decode of the Book of Revelation. Boy, have we been lied to and put in such fear about the End Times. It is clear in this book that the evil, wicked ones are doomed to hell and the righteous should not fear. We have been incorrectly taught both in school and in many churches. Buy, read and have hope! The Lord is in control and HE wins and so do the righteous ones who stand firm with our Lord. These creeps are going down and there will be justice.

Amazon Customer
5.0 out of 5 stars Great read!
Reviewed in the United States on July 27, 2024
Verified Purchase
I bought this book and have read through it twice the last 2 years. Made lots of highlights and marks so I could use it as a reference while reading my Bible and following the current news cycle. It's an easy read and I enjoy getting different perspectives and interpretations on end times events and timelines.

Koalabear1019
5.0 out of 5 stars The TRUTH about the "end" times! It's NOT scary!

Reviewed in the United States on October 1, 2021
Verified Purchase
Melissa has a true servant's heart.
There's no mistaking that she's a straight-shooter who loves the Lord and immensely reveres the Word of God!

If you are looking for a typical Revelation/End times book, this isn't it. This book will challenge most everything you've ever learned about these subjects (especially if it was from a pastor or priest!), and will enlighten you to the evil one's plan that's been playing out ALL OUR LIVES and is culminating now!

Before discovering Melissa, I was searching everywhere for the truth of what we have been experiencing worldwide (digging in the Bible, praying, Internet searches) and the Lord led me to her. She has helped me SO MUCH! Her reassuring and encouraging way of communicating, positive attitude, and great sense of humor can be seen all throughout the book. Any time anxiety creeps in, I hear her say: "Don't worrryyy" and it helps me re-focus. Thank you, Melissa, you are a treasure!

97009939R00129